Adolescent Sexuality: New Challenges for Social Work

The *Journal of Social Work & Human Sexuality* series:

- *Social Work and Child Sexual Abuse*, edited by Jon R. Conte and David A. Shore
- *Human Sexuality in Medical Social Work*, edited by Larry Lister and David A. Shore
- *Homosexuality and Social Work*, edited by Robert Schoenberg and Richard Goldberg, with David A. Shore
- *Feminist Perspectives on Social Work and Human Sexuality*, edited by Mary Valentich and James Gripton
- *Social Work Practice in Sexual Problems*, edited by James Gripton and Mary Valentich
- *Human Sexuality, Ethnoculture and Social Work*, edited by Larry Lister
- *Adolescent Sexualities: Overviews and Principles of Intervention*, edited by Paula Allen-Meares and David A. Shore
- *Intimate Relationships: Some Social Work Perspectives on Love*, edited by Wendell Ricketts and Harvey L. Gochros
- *Infertility and Adoption: A Guide for Social Work Practice*, edited by Deborah Valentine
- *Sociopsychological Aspects of Sexually Transmitted Diseases*, edited by Margaret Rodway and Marianne Wright
- *The Sexually Unusual: Guide to Understanding and Helping*, edited by Dennis M. Dailey
- *Treatment of Sex Offenders in Social Work and Mental Health Settings*, edited by John S. Wodarski and Daniel L. Whitaker
- *Adolescent Sexuality: New Challenges for Social Work*, edited by Paula Allen-Meares and Constance Hoenk Shapiro

Adolescent Sexuality: New Challenges for Social Work

Paula Allen-Meares
Constance Hoenk Shapiro
Editors

Routledge
Taylor & Francis Group
NEW YORK AND LONDON

First published 1989 by The Haworth Press, Inc.

Published 2016 by Routledge
711 Third Avenue, New York, NY 10017
2 Park Square, Milton Park, Abingdon, Oxfordshire OX14 4RN

First issued in paperback 2016

Routledge is an imprint of the Taylor and Francis Group, an informa business

Adolescent Sexuality: New Challenges for Social Work has also been published as *Journal of Social Work & Human Sexuality*, Volume 8, Number 1 1989.

The Haworth Press, Inc., 10 Alice Street, Binghamton, NY 13904-1580
EUROSPAN/Haworth, 3 Henrietta Street, London WC2E 8LU England

Library of Congress Cataloging-in-Publication Data

Adolescent sexuality : new challenges for social work / Paula Allen-Meares. Constance Hoenk Shapiro, editors.
"Has also been published as Journal of social work & human sexuality, volume 8, number 1 1989" – T.p. version.
p. cm.
Bibliography: p.
ISBN 0-86656-901-4
1. Social work with teenagers – United States. 2. Social service and sex – United States. 3. Teenagers – United States – Sexual behavior. I. Allen-Meares, Paula, 1948- II. Shapiro, Constance Hoenk.
HV1431.A635 1989
362.7'96'0973 – dc10 89-1668
CIP

ISBN 13: 978-1-138-96597-3 (pbk)
ISBN 13: 978-0-86656-901-9 (hbk)

Adolescent Sexuality: New Challenges for Social Work

CONTENTS

ADOLESCENT SEXUALITY IN RURAL AND URBAN AMERICA

ABOUT THE EDITORS

Paula Allen-Meares, CSW, MSW, PhD, is Associate Professor at the University of Illinois, School of Social Work, Urbana-Champaign campus. She was coordinator and developer of an in-school program for pregnant adolescents and adolescent parents. She has published and lectured on issues of adolescent sexuality and serves on the Editorial Boards of *Social Work* and *Educational and Psychological Research*.

Constance Hoenk Shapiro, MSW, PhD, is Associate Professor and Director of the Social Work Program of Cornell University, Ithaca, New York. She is the author of *Adolescent Pregnancy Prevention* and *Infertility and Pregnancy Loss*. Further, she has lectured extensively on human sexuality and reproductive health and has many publications to her credit.

Contributors

Paula Allen-Meares, PhD, Associate Professor, School of Social Work, University of Illinois, Urbana, Illinois.

Raymond Berger, MSW, PhD, Professor and Director of Masters Research Thesis, Department of Social Work, California State University, Long Beach, California.

Catherine Chilman, MSW, PhD, Professor Emerita, School of Social Welfare, University of Wisconsin-Milwaukee, Milwaukee, Wisconsin.

Edith Freeman, MSW, PhD, Associate Professor, School of Social Welfare, University of Kansas, Lawrence, Kansas.

Sylvia Hacker, CSE, PhD, Associate Professor, School of Nursing, University of Michigan, Ann Arbor, Michigan.

Dianne F. Harrison, MSW, PhD, Professor, School of Social Work, Florida State University, Tallahassee, Florida.

Gary W. Holden, Research Associate, School of Social Work, Columbia University, New York, New York.

Lucy R. Mercier, MSW, Department of Social Work, California State University, Long Beach, California.

Burton Mindick, PhD, Professor, Department of Sociology, Cornell University, Ithaca, New York.

Michael S. Moncher, Research Associate, School of Social Work, Columbia University, New York, New York.

Andrea Parrot, PhD, Assistant Professor, Department of Human Service Studies at Cornell University, Cornell University, Ithaca, New York.

R. C. Pennell, BS, is a second year MSW student, Florida State University, Tallahassee, Florida.

Steven P. Schinke, PhD, Professor, School of Social Work, Columbia University, New York, New York.

Constance Shapiro, MSW, PhD, Associate Professor, Director of the Social Work Program, Cornell University, Ithaca, New York.

Foreword

The challenges faced by adolescents and their families always include sexual issues. For years, social workers have been at the forefront of efforts to advocate for adolescents who have needed services aimed at prevention or treatment of sexual and reproductive needs. Yet recent years have brought new challenges for professionals who try to help adolescents understand their burgeoning sexuality and to acknowledge the powerful consequences of some sexual behaviors. This collection will address the most compelling issues that social workers face as we leave behind the decade of the 1980s and anticipate the emerging issues in adolescent sexuality for the 1990s. Issues such as AIDS, acquaintance rape, and evolving sex roles add to the challenges social workers face in working with adolescents. In addition, attention to changing environments, particularly urban and rural settings, is crucial for social workers in their efforts to tailor interventions to unique regional needs. Underserved populations, including gay and lesbian adolescents, adolescent fathers, and minorities at high risk for AIDS complement the emphasis in this collection on education as a key to prevention.

Social workers are practiced in dealing with resistance, but nowhere is that dynamic more apparent than in the area of adolescent sexuality. The federal government, well known for its reluctance to fund programs designed at prevention, now faces record numbers of adolescents who need complex treatment services. Resistance can be seen in the family context too. Parents, who themselves were probably inadequately prepared to be helpful sex educators for their children, face new challenges in this era of AIDS and other untreatable sexually transmitted diseases. Parental resistance has historically interfered with some efforts to develop community-based programs, but when such programs include parents in the development and implementation stages, resistance often disappears as parents find their own needs being met by such programs. Adolescents themselves may demonstrate some resistance to programs aimed at helping them with sexual issues, especially at a time that they are caught up in the developmental task of declaring autonomy from parents and rebelling against adults perceived as authority figures in their lives. This is a time when adolescents grapple with confusing feelings as they try to evolve sexual identities that feel reasonable, as they interact with their peers, and as they seek answers to questions with which parents and adult role models may never have grappled.

In addition to issues of resistance, social workers also must be sensitive to rural and urban issues, to needs of special population groups, and to innovative contexts of providing services that will ultimately benefit the adolescent. Well known for their need to declare autonomy from their families, adolescents challenge us as professionals to create room for family involvement that does not stifle their emerging sense of independence. When they feel unsure, threatened, or overwhelmed, adolescents need to view the family as a safe haven in which they can replenish their energies, repair their hurts and resolve their differences. Yet many of the articles in this collection reveal the reluctance of adolescents to confide in their families or to see them as a source of support. Social workers, long accustomed to conceptualizing the "person in situation," must accept the challenge of helping family members, often highly stressed themselves, to balance the needs for autonomy/dependence declared by their adolescent members. In addition, since some families are too overwhelmed to offer the support their adolescents need, several articles in this collection suggest ways that social workers can strengthen and utilize community resources to supplement the flagging energies of some families: the church, family planning agencies, schools, and support groups.

It is our hope that this collection will accomplish several purposes. The first purpose is to highlight the emerging issues that social workers face as we help adolescents define their problems and seek solutions to them. Although adolescent sexuality is a familiar issue for many of us, the new consequences of sexual expression go far beyond the familiar outcomes of unplanned pregnancy, premature parenthood, and treatable sexually transmitted diseases that have occupied our research and practice for so many years.

Now our challenge is broadened to include issues of sexual preference, acquaintance rape, new social roles, and sexually transmitted diseases that may be untreatable and even life-threatening.

The second purpose we hope to accomplish is to emphasize the importance of creativity and client empowerment at a time of skeptical federal support in the area of adolescent sexuality. Preventive efforts have rarely been well funded, in part due to objections that focussed on preventive efforts as encouraging sexual experimentation. Subsequent agreements to fund preventive programs were accompanied by insistence that abstinence receive maximum attention, with minimal information given to the real needs of sexually active adolescents: information on contraception, decision-making methods, and communication skills. Now that the consequences of adolescent sexual activity are potentially more devastating than even a decade ago, social workers will be freed from many of the earlier constraints imposed upon them. We must strive to develop innovative approaches and, in addition to tapping into new funding opportunities that have become available in this era of AIDS, must measure carefully the impact of the interventions, so as to add to the ongoing knowledge of program effectiveness. And, as several articles in this collection emphasize, we must listen carefully to the adolescents whom we purport to serve, since they can be an invaluable resource as we strive to understand their unique issues and the ways in which services can best be designed to meet their pressing needs.

Constance Hoenk Shapiro
Paula Allen-Meares

CHALLENGES

Some Major Issues Regarding Adolescent Sexuality and Childbearing in the United States

Catherine S. Chilman

SUMMARY. Adolescent sexuality is a complex developmental process strongly affected by both familial and societal systems. Major research findings regarding adolescent coitus, contraception, and childbearing are summarized. More emphasis on the positive, rather than problematic, aspects of teenage sexuality is advocated as well as broadened social work roles in treatment, social action and research.

SOME BASIC CONCEPTS

Adolescence

Adolescence is defined as that period in a person's life that stretches from the onset of puberty to young adulthood. Puberty refers to the first phase of adolescence when sexual maturation becomes evident. Entrance into young adulthood is less easily defined. For the purposes of this essay, however, age 18 will be used.

Adolescence is often seen as consisting of two major stages. The first stretches from the onset of puberty to about ages 14 through 16; psychologically, it is characterized by the push for independence from parents and attempts to resolve conflicts between the continuing need for childish dependence and the desire for a separate identity. The second stage is marked by the search for a mature identity,

---

Catherine S. Chilman's recent major books include *Adolescent Sexuality in a Changing American Society: Perspectives for Human Service Professionals* (1983) and *Families in Trouble* (co-editor and author), a five volume series (1988).

the quest for a mate, and the exploration of different sets of values and of occupational and other life goals. Throughout adolescence, sexuality is the major theme, as the young person grows toward womanhood or manhood, with the many roles and functions of becoming a feminine or masculine adult.

Human sexuality is often described as including the physical characteristics and capacities for specific sex behaviors, together with psychosocial learning, values, norms, and attitudes about these behaviors. This definition is broadened here to include a sense of gender identity and related concepts, behaviors, and attitudes about the self and others in the context of both the family system and the larger society. According to this definition, sexuality pervades virtually every aspect of the person's life. It is affected by the totality of what it means to be a male or female person; by one's past and present experiences and anticipations of the future; by one's stage of development and life situation; by one's physical-constitutional capacities and characteristics; by the kind of society in which one lives, as well as the historical background of that society with its particular views regarding adolescence and human sexuality over the generations (Chilman, 1983, 1988).

Needed: A Family and Societal Systems Approach

Most of the past and current practice, program, and research efforts regarding adolescent sexuality have focused on its problematic aspects, especially adolescent pregnancy and childbearing. These emphases have failed to pay sufficient attention to the important broader dimensions. For instance, as defined above, adolescent sexuality should be viewed as a central aspect of young people's overall development, within the systems of both their families and within the larger society.

It should also be viewed in terms of its positive potentialities as well as its problematic ones. There appear to be no generally accepted criteria for healthy adolescent sexuality. On the basis of considerable theory, research, and observation, I will suggest the following. Healthy sexuality includes gradual growth toward a clear sense of identity and toward an acceptance of the self as a valuable, valued young female or male. It includes a growing sense of personal and interpersonal competence as a sexual person, broadly defined. It also includes a general understanding of the psychobiology of both sexes and of reproductive and family planning processes. The contribution of sexuality to fulfillment of the self and others should also be generally and increasingly understood. This includes the capacity to derive sexual gratification through individual and interpersonal activities in a relational context: a context that is characterized by freedom for self-expression within clearly defined limits. These limits include appropriate use of protection from unwanted pregnancies and sexually transmitted disease.

This definition may seem overly idealistic. Note that emphasis is placed on *gradual* growth towards these attitudes and behaviors as the young person moves from childhood to early adolescence to later adolescent stages to adulthood. In doing so the young person slowly leaves behind such well-documented characteristics of early adolescence as an uncertain sense of personal identity, low ego strength, narcissism, dependence on external rather than internal means of impulse control, poor capacity for responsible behavior and limited ability to foresee probable future outcomes of present actions (Loevinger, 1966; Kohlberg & Gilligan, 1972; Marcia, 1978; Elkind, 1967; Adelson, 1975; Erikson 1968; Chilman, 1983 and 1986).

It can be seen that healthy adolescent sexuality, as defined here, is unlikely to develop through sex education efforts alone, whether at home, church or school. Rather, such attitudes, feelings and behaviors more centrally develop gradually, from birth onward, in the context of both the family system and the larger society.

Family systems theory, as used here, views families as open ecological systems, heavily affected by multi-generational interpersonal dynamics as well as by interactions with the larger environment. Thus, the multi-generational experiences, values, beliefs, attitudes, and behaviors of each family member affect all family members in a host of overt and covert ways. Moreover, changing social, economic, and political conditions in the larger environment have multiple effects on families as they move through time. In turn, familial attitudes and behaviors have numerous effects on many aspects of the environment (Chilman, Nunnally & Cox, 1988).

The functioning of family systems (including the sexuality of their members) is also affected by family structure (such as one-parent, two-parent, never-married, divorced or remarried families), family size, number and spacing of children, and stage of family development such as mid-stage when children are adolescent and parents are middle-aged (Carter & McGoldrick, 1980). The sexuality of each family member, as defined earlier, is an important component in the development and behavior of each of these members including children and adolescents.

The multiple effects of the larger society vary from family to family and from individual to individual. This variation depends on many things including race, ethnicity, religion, socioeconomic status and place of residence. The dominant culture of today (1988) may be defined as chiefly materialistic, self-centered, hedonistic, competitive, and violent. The social revolution of the 1960s, which included an overdue sexual revolution swept away many outworn repressive norms. Starting as an equalitarian movement for improved community life, it shifted during the 1970s and even more so in the 1980s to a splintered society in which the private good became primary and the public good of little account. Traditional norms, beliefs, and values have been largely discarded and we have yet to evolve a new set of guidelines to take the place of the old ones. We are surrounded by threats of thermonuclear war; air and water pollution; mounting corruption in government, industry and business; and a pervasive mass media that becomes ever more unrestrained in its portrayal of violence and sex. Sexual activities are depicted as completely rewarding, with no mention made of possible pregnancies or sexually transmitted diseases; no mention made of the importance of contraception or of responsible committed human relationships. We also live in an insecure two-tier economy with rising riches for the fortunate and increasing poverty for others.

All of these trends are undermining such social institutions as families, schools, neighborhoods, communities, religious organizations, and the social fabric of businesses and industries. It is a society in which hope and trust are hard to come by. This society is apt to have a particularly adverse effect on adolescents who are just moving into the adult world and are becoming increasingly aware of the troubled, as well as tempting, society they are inheriting. All things considered, it seems remarkable that so many teenagers appear to do so well, rather than that a number of them get into various kinds of difficulty, including, in some instances, unplanned parenthood.

Although I have argued here that we should emphasize positive, rather than problematic, adolescent sexuality, it is appropriate to briefly review some of the salient aspects of behaviors leading to teen-age parenting along with its apparent consequences. This is partly because the topic is important, in itself, and partly because most of the research regarding adolescent sexuality is on this subject. Recent important studies are emphasized here.

ADOLESCENT PARENTHOOD

Trends

Contrary to widespread publicity and common assumptions, the nationwide birthrate for adolescent women declined more or less steadily between 1970 and 1984 (the last date for which birth statistics are available, 1988). In 1970, this rate was about 9% of all teenage women, but it had dropped to about 5.3% in 1982. The birth rate for black adolescent women in 1984 was twice as high as the rate for whites. However, the difference between the two races was smaller than it had been in earlier years. Although the birthrate and numbers of births declined between 1970 and 1983, the pregnancy rate rose somewhat. A 40% rate of abortion for teen pregnancies was a leading reason for the decline in births (Chilman, 1988).

The rate of *nonmarital* pregnancies and parenthood rose markedly between 1970 and 1983 from one third all births to adolescents in 1970 to more than one half in the early 1980s. Black adolescents were far more likely than whites to have nonmarital births: 89% of births to black adolescents compared to 45% of births to Hispanic teenage women and 34% to non-Hispanic whites in 1984. The chief reasons for these differences are discussed in a later section.

Incidence of Coitus

Rates of nonmarital intercourse among women, ages 15-19, increased sharply between 1967 (at the height of the social and sexual revolutions) and 1976. There was a slight decline in these rates between 1979 and 1982, perhaps reflecting a general national trend toward conservatism. In general, participation in intercourse rises with the young person's age, with about 5% of young women reporting intercourse experience before age 15 compared to nearly half by age 19 (Chilman, 1983; Zelnik & Kantner, 1980; Hayes, 1987).

Data for young men are less reliable than for young women for a variety of reasons, including the fact that it is more difficult for researchers to reach them. However, the best (albeit somewhat flawed) data available suggest that in 1979, by age 19, over three-fourths of white males and almost all black males had participated in coitus. By age 20, most unmarried men and women are sexually active and the earlier higher rates of males tend to disappear (Hayes, 1987).

Differences in rates between black and white teenagers are largely, if not completely, accounted for by differences in the socioeconomic status of the two groups, with far more black than white adolescents coming from families with low income and low educational-occupational status of parents. When controls are used for SES effects, rates of adolescent intercourse among young women of both races becomes quite similar (*CDF Reports*, April, 1988).

Adolescent sexual behaviors, like other characteristics and behaviors of young people, are highly variable, with large within-group differences (Hayes, 1987; Chilman, 1983; Furstenberg et al., 1987). Sexually active adolescents differ among themselves in many ways, such as ages at sexual initiation; frequency of intercourse; kinds of activities; numbers of partners, nature of the total relationship; attitudes, feelings and reactions to the sex activity; apparent reasons for these activities; use or non-use of contraceptives; total life situation of adolescents within their families and the community; and so on.

If more researchers looked for variations *within* their data, rather than at over-all group averages alone, they would probably find a number of subgroups of adolescents for whom differing styles and correlates of behavior would pertain. (See, for example, the discussion of recent research by Furstenberg et al., in a later section.) Despite the problems of using only group averages and in combining a large number of different kinds of studies in one presentation, it should be useful to examine Table I for clues to further understanding of early nonmarital intercourse.

Clearly, all of the factors presented here could not apply to any one adolescent or any one subgroup of adolescents, as the foregoing remarks suggest. Moreover, it is not appropriate to view all nonmarital adolescent coitus as problematic. As my earlier definition of healthy adolescent sexuality implies, teenagers (especially older ones) who engage in nonmarital intercourse in the context of a committed caring relationship and with adequate contraceptive and health protections, may well be expressing positive psychosexual development. *Not* engaging in sexual activities of this sort *could* be a symptom of an overly inhibited, withdrawn psychosexual orientation, depending on the age and total life situation of the young person.

Moving to an inspection of factors presented in Table I, we see that only one small study deals with family system characteristics. This is partly because few researchers trained in psychology or sociology are well acquainted with family systems theory, despite the fact that some family social scientists and therapists have made significant theoretical and methodological advances in this field over the past 20 years. (See, for example, Haley, 1980; Minuchin & Fishman, 1981; McGoldrick, Pearce & Giordano, 1982; Bowen, 1978; Hartman & Laird, 1987.) Then, too, family systems characteristics, especially as they may change over the family development cycle, are exceptionally difficult to measure. A global measure of family functioning which is well standardized and relatively simple to administer does not now exist. (For an excellent discussion of this complex topic, see Weiss & Jacobs, 1988.) The family-related factors that do appear in Table I include single parent status, mother having been a teenage parent, dysfunctional family system (one small clinical study), large family size, permissive attitudes of parents and conflict with parents.

This author's acquaintance with the case histories of the overall

TABLE I

Major Factors Apparently Associated with Nonmarital Intercourse Among Adolescents: A Summary of Research Findings

Factors	Males	Females
Social Situation		
Not living in a middle-class, family-focussed neighborhood	yes	yes
Parents having less than a college education	unknown	yes, especially for blacks
Low level of religiousness	yes	yes, especially for whites
Norms favoring equality between the sexes	probably	yes
Permissive sexual norms of the larger society and reference group	yes	yes
Racism and poverty	yes	yes
Migration from rural to urban areas	unknown	yes
High youth unemployment	yes	yes, especially for blacks

Peer-group pressure	yes	not clear
Lower social class	yes	yes
Sexually active friends	yes	yes
Single-parent (usually low-income) family, especially if parent is dating	unknown	yes
Mother having been a teenage parent	unknown	yes(a)
Large family size	yes	yes
Psychological		
Early use of tobacco, drugs and alcohol	yes	yes
Low self-esteem	no[a]	yes[a]
Desire for affection	no[a]	yes[a]
Dysfunctional family system	unknown	yes[a]
Low educational goals and poor educational achievement	yes	yes
Low-tested intelligence	yes	yes
Alienation	no[a]	yes[a]
Deviant attitudes	yes	yes
High social criticism	no[a]	yes[a]
Permissive attitudes of parents	yes[a]	yes[a]
Conflict with parents	yes[a]	yes[a]

Table I (continued)

Factors	Males	Females
Going steady; being in love	yes[a]	yes[a]
Steady love partner with permissive attitudes		
Risk-taking attitudes	yes[a]	yes[a]
Passivity and dependence	no[a]	yes[a]
Aggression; high levels of activity	yes	no[a]
Biological		
Older than 16	yes	yes
Early puberty, especially for whites	yes	yes

[a]Variables supported by only one or two small studies. Other variables are supported by a number of investigations. The major studies on which this table is based are: Furstenberg (1976); Jessor and Jessor (1975); Sorenson (1973); Kantner and Zelnik (1972); Udry et al. (1975); Simon et al. (1972); Zelnik and Kantner (1977); Fox (1980); Cvetkovich and Grote (1975); Schulz, et al. 1977; Presser (1978); Zelnik, (1980); DeLameter and MacCorquodale, (1979); Mindick and Oskamp (1982); Zelnik, Kantner and Ford, (1982); Furstenberg and Crawford (1978); Reiss andMiller (1979); Peterson, Moore, Furstenberg and Morgan (1985); Thornton (1985); Hagan, Astone and Kitigawa (1985); Hayes (1987); Mott (9183); Hagan and Kitigawa (1983); Jessor et al. (1983); Newcomer and Udry (1983).

development of many adolescents strongly suggests that other familial factors, including family system characteristics, are often associated with an adolescent's early participation in nonmarital intercourse without contraceptive protection. These factors include alcoholism on the part of one or both parents, family violence, incest, severe conflict in parental marriage, chronic physical or mental illness on the part of a parent or sibling, authoritarian and punitive parents (or parent), low family communication, conflict-ridden and/or rigid family systems, families with ambiguous boundaries, and neglecting or rejecting parents. More or less the opposite family characteristics have been frequently observed among those adolescents who abstain from nonmarital coitus until after age 18 or who engage in coitus only in the context of a steady relationship and only with adequate contraceptive protection. It is my strong impression that family factors such as those described above have not been found by researchers studying adolescent sexual behaviors largely because pertinent questions have not been asked to any large extent.

Turning back to Table I, we see that the social milieu of adolescents has been studied rather more thoroughly. In particular, note that a number of investigations have revealed the strong influence of highly permissive social norms, racism, poverty, migration, unemployment, and disorganized neighborhoods.

In terms of psychological characteristics, it is impressive that poor school performance and low academic goals are found, in study after study, to have an outstanding relationship to early sex activity. Since, aside from families, schools are the central influence in the lives of most young people, their ability to perform well academically and the ability of schools to meet their needs are of tremendous importance. Low achievement in school, especially when it is combined with problem situations at home, is apt to undermine a young person's self-esteem, her/his acceptance by the dominant peer group, and her/his hopes for future educational-occupational success. Without high self-esteem, acceptance by the major peer group, and hopes for the future, an adolescent is much more vulnerable to such easy impulse gratification and escapist behaviors as early nonmarital coitus along with heavy use of drugs and alcohol (evidence is growing that substance abuse and early unprotected coitus, and poor use of contraceptives are frequently linked [Mindick & Oskamp, 1982; Jessor et al., 1983]). The above behaviors are apt to be particularly true when they are also modeled within a teenager's family.[1]

Contraceptive Use

It is well-known that many sexually active adolescents fail to use effective contraceptives or use them inconsistently. Space constraints forbid a detailed presentation of the research associated with these tendencies. However, the same general patterns appear as those presented in Table I. Ready availability of high quality, low-cost contraceptives is an important added factor. Contraceptive behavior may be changing recently through increased use of the condom as a protection against AIDS. (See the article on this topic in this collection.) In brief, it seems clear that adolescents who feel good about themselves, and have high self-esteem, plus clear expectations for their future educational-occupational success, are less likely than others to engage in early nonmarital coitus or, if they do so engage, they are more likely to consistently use reliable contraceptives.

This observation is bolstered by recent research reported by Abramse, Morrison, and White (1988), who found that willingness to consider unmarried parenthood was associated with self-reports of disciplinary problems and absenteeism in school, low academic achievement and goals, plus depressive tendencies (among Anglo whites and Hispanics but not among blacks).

Reports of recent studies by the Alan Guttmacher Institute provide important information concerning pregnancy, contraception and family planning services in a number of countries (Jones et al., 1988). The United States has higher rates of pregnancy, abortion, and childbearing than do most other developed countries, especially those in western Europe. An earlier study had shown this was true for teenagers but the recent research shows this is also the case for

---

1. Space constraints prevent further discussion here of the numerous theories posed by psychoanalytically and personality oriented scholars regarding psychosexual development of children and adolescents and sexual activities as a reflection of a host of processes within and between persons. (See, for instance, Chilman, 1983, 1986.)

older women, especially those under age 25. (Other groups of U.S. women increasingly rely on sterilization as their preferred method of birth control.)

Free of low-cost family planning services are more widely available to all socioeconomic groups in most countries than in the U.S. where specialized family planning clinics are primarily established to serve the poor. Moreover, contraceptives in most of the western democracies are provided through general medical services as part of a total health program rather than through obstetricians-gynecologists as is the chief approach in the United States. Unlike this country, information about contraception is readily available in the schools and in the mass media in most of the nations studied: the subject is seen as a natural, accepted part of human life, rather than as something secret and deviant, as in this country. All in all, it appears that contraception has become a readily accepted part of the national culture in many nations and its provision has been thoroughly incorporated into both public and private general health care systems. The U.S. approach appears to be lagging behind that of other developed democracies and seems to be encumbered by traditional attitudes and beliefs. High rates of unplanned pregnancies, abortions, and unwanted parenthood for teenagers, as well as for older women, are at least partially a result of our pervasive anxiety about sexuality and contraception, not to mention entrenched interests of medical and related professions. Family planning systems in the U.S. and elsewhere are complex topics with numerous psychological, biological, economic, political, and religious components that require careful consideration far beyond the scope of the present essay.

Abortion

As mentioned earlier, nearly 40% of teenage pregnancies are terminated by abortion (Hayes, 1987). As in the case of participation in early nonmarital coitus and poor or nonuse of contraceptives, young women who are black, of low socioeconomic status, and who have few prospects of obtaining advanced education plus a good job, are less likely than their more advantaged sisters to obtain an abortion. An added reason for this may be that public funding of abortions is no longer available in many states and the private costs are high. Other factors pertain to cultural norms, familial and peer attitudes, and the like.

Male Partners of Teenage Mothers

Marsiglio (1987) has provided some helpful information about teenage fathers in his analyses of data from the National Longitudinal Survey of the Labor Experience of Youth. According to this analysis, 7% of young males, ages 20-27, in 1984 said they had fathered a child when they were teenagers. Marsiglio warns that this figure may be inaccurate because the respondents may have been less than completely candid. Then, too, they wouldn't necessarily know whether or not they had fathered a child.

More than three-fourths of the children of these young fathers were born outside of marriage. Many of the fathers were also high school dropouts. Young black men were especially apt to have been responsible for a nonmarital birth. Only 15% of these young black unmarried fathers said they lived with their partners after the child's birth compared to 48% of Hispanics, 58% of disadvantaged whites, and 77% of nondisadvantaged whites.

There are various probable causes for the rise in adolescent *nonmarital* childbearing in recent years. In general, social norms have become more permissive concerning births outside of marriage. Norms have been less punitive and rigid on this topic among low-income blacks for many years and are probably becoming even more flexible in line with current social trends. Then, too, other factors particularly affect the black population. Over two-thirds of this population live in families with incomes at or below the poverty line. Thus, there are few financial resources for marriages of adolescent parents. Unemployment rates are particularly high and increasing for black youth, both males and females. As of 1982, only one-third of young black men under age 20 held regular jobs, contrasted to about two-thirds of young white men (Wilson & Neckerman, 1986). Moreover, there are far more young females than males in the black population. This is largely a result of high rates of homicide, accidents and incarceration in jails or prisons among young black males. Chiefly as a result of their larger numbers in the population, many young black women cannot find black husbands. Therefore, young men may form sexual relationships with a number of unmarried women and father the children of several temporary mates (Farley, 1980; Blumstein, 1982).

The problems of many black adolescent mothers, financial and otherwise, would not necessarily be solved or even markedly reduced if they married since so many of the young males involved are unemployed or under-employed (Hayes, 1987; Chilman, 1988). Moreover, attempts to reduce the financial problems of many unmarried (or separated or divorced) adolescent mothers through the enforcement of support payments from young fathers would frequently meet with meager success because so few of these fathers (especially black ones) are employed at adequate wages.

Outcomes of Adolescent Childbearing

This is a large, complex topic, beyond the scope of the present essay. Suffice it to say here that the outcomes of little education, unemployment, poverty, welfare dependency, and large family size often ascribed to adolescent parenthood, per se, may have occurred for many of these young people, in any case, because of the vulnerabilities (on the average) within themselves and within their families plus the inequities of the larger society in which so many of them live.[2] Adding parenthood to their pre-existing problems would probably *increase* the difficulties of these young people, but would not, in many instances, be a *primary* and sole cause of the educational, employment, financial and other difficulties so many of them face.

Furstenberg et al. (1987), report on their outstanding 17-year follow-up study of a mostly black group of Baltimore women who had been teenage mothers in 1966 (Furstenberg, 1976). The authors emphasize the tremendous variability of their group and warn against stereotyping the so-called consequences of adolescent parenthood. Impressively, these investigators found that many important changes gradually occurred for the mother and their children over

2. This is a tentative conclusion reached by the author but many scholars in the field would disagree with her in whole or part. See Furstenberg et al., 1987, for a highly competent discussion of these issues.

the 17-year period. For example, over 70% of the mothers had completed high school by 1983 (in contrast to 10% high school graduation in 1966) and 5% had graduated from college.

Thirty percent were currently married which is fairly close to the 1983 national average for black women in their age group. Average family size (2.3 children) was also near the national average for black women. About 30% had received welfare in the past year, again, close to the national average for their group. Average income levels were also similar to the average.

The rate of employment for these mothers rose steadily over the 17 years, with 72% being employed in 1982, although most of them were working in unskilled or semi-skilled jobs and receiving quite low wages. The authors sum up their findings in this part of their study by remarking on the extreme variability of the group, the many changes in their lives over the 17-year period, and the fact that, on the average, they were considerably, but not extremely, behind otherwise comparable women who had not been adolescent mothers.

Important personal factors that contributed to the later life success of some of the women were: parental supports, positive role models, academic competence, strong educational-occupational motivation, school and health (including family planning) assistance programs, limited further fertility, and stable marriages to employed men. The investigators, along with a number of others, also stress the importance of job training and employment opportunities as escapes from poverty.

Although the mass media and some professionals emphasize the highly adverse effects of teenage parents on their youngsters, much of the research evidence has failed to support this generalization as it applies to *young* children. However, the Furstenberg et al. (1987) 17-year follow-up study, plus data from the National Survey of Children, indicated that by the time children born to adolescent mothers became teenagers themselves, they were especially apt to have academic and behavior problems in school, with half of this group having repeated a grade compared to one-fifth of the children of mothers who were demographically comparable but who had not had children until they were older.

The Baltimore follow-up study showed highly variable forms of maternal care and developmental outcomes for the teenage youngsters but the interviewers found little apparent child abuse or neglect and a great deal of maternal love and pride in their sons and daughters. It seems unfortunate that so many researchers and others emphasize the material disadvantages that often accompany early parenthood without taking into account the psychosocial positives that children can bring to their parents—positives such as love and affirmation of the self as uniquely valued human beings.

The sexual behaviors of the teenage youngsters of women who had been adolescent mothers were also studied. Nearly half of the girls and almost all of the boys reportedly had experienced intercourse by age 15. This is fairly similar to the rates reported for black 15-year-old girls in a nationwide 1979 survey (Zelnik & Kantner, 1980). (Comparable data for males are missing.) The likelihood of a girl's having had intercourse by age 15 in the Furstenberg et al. study (1987) was increased by her having an unmarried mother who was on welfare, not in school and the parent of large numbers of children. Despite their high rates of intercourse, only 11% of the adolescents reportedly had a pregnancy by age 15 or 16 and none had become parents (presumably pregnancies were terminated by miscarriages or abortions). It was not clear to what extent the mothers of these teenagers had given them *explicit* contraceptive information though many said they had warned their youngsters to "protect themselves" if they had coitus.

The authors of the Baltimore studies show commendable imagination, scholarship, and expertise in attempting to chart the life courses of both the mothers and their children over the 17-year period of their studies. It is impossible to do justice to the details and important discussion of their findings in this brief essay. Rather, interested readers are urged to carefully study the entire report (Furstenberg et al., 1987).

Commentary

It appears to this writer that teenage childbearing as a social and economic issue has been overemphasized by many sectors of our society. For example, it has become popular to blame high welfare costs on teenage childbearing per se. However, a careful examination of research related to the subject leads to the recognition that structural problems in the society itself—unemployment, low wages, racism, inequities of income distribution, poor inner city schools, inadequate health services, and poor housing all combine to largely account for poverty and economic dependency. These adverse factors, themselves, are often causes rather than outcomes of nonmarital early childbearing. It is simpler and, I suggest, more appealing to many adults to blame welfare costs on the sex behavior of adolescents rather than on basic social and economic deficiencies that are exceptionally expensive and difficult to solve—particularly demanding of economic sacrifices through taxes, and the like, on the part of the well-to-do.

Of course, unplanned, unwanted childbearing is often a problem, but it can be a problem for people of many ages, not for teenagers alone. It is important to provide a range of services aimed at *preventing*, at any age, problems of unplanned, unwanted parenthood if possible (especially a range of birth control and related services) and at providing needed assistance to those parents who are problem-laden. Note that Furstenberg et al. (1987) found that those former adolescent parents who escaped from poverty were more likely than others to have had many forms of assistance: familial support, educational-occupational opportunities, health and social services, and stable marriages to employed men, plus their own individual abilities and strong motivations for financial success.

All in all, it seems more appropriate to emphasize the needs of *all* adolescents in our society, not just the 5% of teenage women who become unmarried mothers in a given year. So much noisy attention and provision of special services for this group sends a message to teenagers, in general—if you want adults to be concerned about your needs, become a teenage mother (rather less so, a teenage father). If pregnancy isn't your "thing," try substance abuse or delinquency, or even AIDS. If you don't have problems that are upsetting and costly to society, don't expect much help or attention from the adult world: a world that seems basically hostile toward, and distrustful of, adolescents.

SOME IMPLICATIONS FOR SOCIAL WORKERS

The research and theory review and suggestions presented above have a number of implications for social workers; only some of these implications can be sketched within the confines of this paper. To promote "healthy" adolescent sexuality, as defined earlier, and to prevent or treat some of its problematic aspects, a number of activities are indicated.

At the direct practice level, it is important to work with adolescent youth within the context and needs of themselves, their families, and their environmental situation. It should be useful to further develop family practice skills that include family systems ecological perspectives plus insights from various other fields, including family therapy. Attention should be paid to the needs, characteristics, and behaviors of all members of the family system. This may include communication patterns, childrearing behaviors, marital relationships, multi-generational issues, developmental stages of family members, family size and structure, transition concerns and special problems such as chemical dependencies, incest, interpersonal conflicts, physical or mental illness and the like. Family treatment strategies often also require attention to the so-called "reality needs" that family members may have in such areas as employment, income assistance, educational and vocational opportunities, health services, and housing.

In working with adolescents and their families, it is important for social workers to think through their own definition of healthy adolescent sexuality and what it may mean to themselves as well as to others. It is essential for them to be clear about their own beliefs and values, avoid traditional stereotypes, and see each individual and family in unique and valid terms.

Attention to the environmental needs of people often requires action at planning, program and policy levels in respect to local, state, and federal provisions for families and their members. It is important that concerned social workers join with others in organized political action to reverse many of the assaults on social programs perpetrated by the Reagan Administration. Especially under OBRA (the Omnibus Budget and Reconstruction Act of 1981), severe cuts were made in such essential programs as family income assistance (AFDC), food and housing subsidies, job training, employment, child care, and support of physical and mental health programs. At federal, state, and local levels, conservative political groups continue to push for restrictions of family planning funds and the right to choices for abortion. (This is especially the case for the rights of adolescents.) Then, too, cuts in Title XX programs have drastically reduced provisions for family counseling services. The same is true of Medicaid in many states. In fact, in numerous communities, family counseling services no longer exist, or are severely limited, for low-income people who do not have health insurance coverage that includes family services.

Thus, at both the societal and family levels, people with limited incomes have been pushed, through government actions, into progressively more adverse conditions since 1980. This, combined with drastic shifts in the economy which have abolished many well-paying industrial jobs and opened up, in their place, service positions with low pay, have created a crisis situation for many families and their members. Children and youth, especially those in disadvantaged minority groups, have suffered the most severely (CDF Reports, 1986-88).

The time is more than overdue for social workers, among others, to recommit themselves to enlightened social policies particularly addressed to the needs of those who are in the lower sector of our increasingly two-tier society—a society that is inherently fragmented and unjust: a society in which "healthy adolescent sexuality," among other components of life, becomes virtually impossible for a large number of our young women and men.

Less dramatically, but still essentially, it is important for social workers, among others, to increase their involvement with research, in both its basic and applied aspects and as both providers and consumers. For example, this essay should demonstrate the usefulness of research in understanding some aspects of human (including adolescent) sexuality in a familial and societal context. We also need more sophisticated practice and program evaluation in our attempts to devise and implement effective policies. Without such evidence it is difficult to "sell" social reform in an "accountability" age such as the present.

REFERENCES

Abramse, A., Morrison, P., & Waite, S. (1988). Teenagers willing to consider single parenthood: Who is at greatest risk? *Family Planning Perspectives*, *20*(1), 13-18.

Adelson, J. (1975). The development of ideology in adolescence. In S. Dragastin, & G. Elder (Eds.), *Adolescence and the life cycle*. New York: John Wiley & Sons.

Blumstein, A. (1982). On the racial disproportion of United States prison populations. *Journal of Criminal Law and Criminology*, *73*, 1259-1281.

Bowen, M. (1978). *Family therapy in clinical practice*. New York: Jason Aronson.

Carter, E., & McGoldrick, M. (Eds.), 1980. *The Family Life Cycle*. New York: Gardner Press.

CDF Reports. (1986-1988). The monthly newsletter of the Child Defense Fund, 122 C Street N.W., Washington, DC. All issues, 1986-1988 contain pertinent information regarding legislative trends affecting children, youth, and their families.

CDF Reports. (1988, April). Piecing together the teen pregnancy puzzle. *9*(10), pp. 1-6. (The monthly newsletter of the Child Defense Fund.)

Chilman, C. (1986). Adolescent heterosexual behaviors. In R. Feldman, & A. Stiffman (Eds.), *Advances in adolescent mental health* (Vol. I, pp. 205-275). Greenwich, CT: JAI Press.

Chilman, C. (1983). *Adolescent sexuality in a changing American society: Social and psychological perspectives for the human services professions*. New York: Wiley & Sons.

Chilman, C. (1988). Disturbed parent-child relationships. In E. Nunnally, C. Chilman, & F. Cox (Eds.), *Families in trouble* (Vol. III). Beverly Hills: Sage.

Chilman, C. (1988). Reproductive norms and the social control of women. In J. Figueira-McDanough, & R. Sarri (Eds.), *The trapped woman* (pp. 34-52). Beverly Hills: Sage.

Chilman, C. (1988). Single adolescent parents. In C. Chilman, E. Nunnally, & F. Cox (Eds.), *Families in trouble* (Vol. V). Beverly Hills: Sage.

Chilman, C., Nunnally, E., & Cox, F. (1988). Preface. In *Families in trouble* (Vol. I). Beverly Hills: Sage.

Cvetkovich, G. & Grote, B. (1975). Antecedents of responsible family formation. Progress report paper presented at a conference sponsored by the Population Division, National Institute of Child Health and Human Development, Bethesda, MD.

DeLameter, J. & MacCorquodale, M. (1979). *Premarital sexuality: Attitudes, relationships, behaviors*. Madison: University of Wisconsin Press.

Elkind, D. (1967). Egocentrism in adolescence. *Child Development*, *38*(4), 1025-1034.

Erikson, E. (1968). *Identity: Youth and crisis*. New York: W.W. Norton.

Farley, R. (1980). Homicide trends in the United States. *Demography*, *17*, 177-188.

Fox, G. (1980). The mother-adolescent daughter relationship as a sexual socialization structure: A research review. *Family Relations*, *29*, 21-28.

Furstenberg, F. & Crawford, A. (1978). Family support: Helping teenage mothers to cope. *Family Planning Perspectives*, *10*, 322-333.

Furstenberg, F., Brooks-Gunn, J., & Morgan, S. (1987). *Adolescent mothers in later life*. Cambridge, MA: Cambridge University Press.

Furstenberg, F., Jr. (1976). *Unplanned parenthood: The social consequences of teenage childbearing*. New York: Free Press.

Haley, A. (1980). *Leaving home*. New York: McGraw-Hill.

Hartman, A. & Laird, J. (1987). Family practice. In *The Encyclopedia of Social Work*. Silver Spring, MD: National Association of Social Workers.

Hayes, C. (Ed.). (1987). *Risking the future: Adolescent sexuality, pregnancy and childbearing*. Washington, DC: National Academy Press.

Hofferth, S. & Hayes, C. (1987). *Risking the future* (Vol. II). Washington, DC: National Academy Press.

Hogan, D., Astone, N., & Kitagawa, E. (1985). Social and environmental factors influencing contraceptive use among black adolescents. *Family Planning Perspectives*, *17*(4), 165-168.

Janzen, C. & Harris, O. (1980). *Family treatment in social work practice*. Itasca, IL: Peacock.

Jessor, R., Costa, E., Jessor, S., & Donovan, J. (1983). The time of first intercourse: A prospective study. *Journal of Personality and Social Psychology*, *44*, 608-626.

Jessor, S. & Jessor, R. (1975). Transition from virginity to nonvirginity among youth: A social-psychological study over time. *Developmental Psychology*, *11*(April), 473-484.

Jones, E., Forrest, J., Henshaw, S., Silverman, J., & Torres, A. (1988). Unintended pregnancy, contraceptive practice and family planning services in developed countries. *Family Planning Perspectives*, *20*(2), 53-67.

Kantner, J. & Zelnik, M. (1972). Sexual experiences of young unmarried women in the U.S. *Family Planning Perspectives*, *4*(4), 9-17.

Kohlberg, L. & Gilligan, C. (1972). The adolescent as a philosopher: The discovery of self in a post conventional world. In J. Kagan, & R. Coles (Eds.), *Twelve to sixteen*. Toronto: George J. McLead.

Loevinger, J. (1976). *Ego development*. San Francisco: Jossey-Bass.

Marcia, J. (1978). Identity in adolescence. In J. Adelson (Ed.), *Handbook of Adolescent Psychology*. New York: John Wiley & Sons.

Marsiglio, W. (1987). Adolescent fathers in the United States: Their initial living arrangements, marital experience and educational outcomes. *Family Planning Perspectives*, *19*(6), 240-251.

McGoldrick, M., Pearce, J., & Giordano, J. (Eds.). (1982). *Ethnicity and family therapy*. New York: Guilford Press.

Mindick, B. & Oskamp, S. (1982). Individual differences among adolescent contraceptors: Some implications for intervention. In I.R. Stuart & C.F. Wells (Eds.), *Pregnancy in adolescence: Needs, problems and management*. New York: Van Nostrand Reinhold.

Minuchin, S. & Fishman, H. (1981). *Family therapy techniques*. Cambridge, MA: Harvard University Press.

Newcomer, S. & Udry, J. (1985). Parent-child Communication and Adolescent Sexual Behavior. *Family Planning Perspectives*, *17*(4), 169-174.

Presser, H. (1978). Age at menarche, socio-sexual behavior and fertility. *Social Biology*, *2*(summer), 94-101.

Reiss, I. & Miller, B. (1979). Heterosexual permissiveness: A theoretical analysis. In W. Burr, R. Hill, I. Nye, & I. Reiss (Eds.), *Contemporary theories about family* (Vol. 1). New York: Free Press.

Schulz, B., Bohrnstedt, G., Borgatta, E., & Evans, R. (1977). Explaining premarital intercourse among college students: A causal model. *Social Forces*, *56*(Sept.), 148-165.

Simon, W., Berger, A., & Gagnon, J. (1972). Beyond anxiety and fantasy: The coital experience of college youths. *Journal of Youth and Adolescence*, *1*(3), 203-222.

Sorenson, R. (1973). *Adolescent sexuality in a contemporary America*. New York: World.

Thornton, A. (1986). Family and institutional factors in adolescent sexuality. Final Report. Institute of Social Research. Ann Arbor, MI.

Udry, J., Bauman, K., & Morris, N. (1975). Changes in premarital coital experience of recent decades of birth cohorts of urban America. *Journal of Marriage and the Family*, *37*(4), 783-787.

Weiss, H. & Jacobs, F. (Eds.). (1988). *Evaluating family programs*. New York: Aldine.

Wilson, W. & Neckerman, K. (1986). Poverty and family structure. In S. Danziger & D. Weingerg (Eds.), *Fighting poverty*. Cambridge, MA: Harvard University Press.

Zelnik, M. (1980). Determinants of fertility behavior among U.S. females aged 15-19, 1971 and 1976. Final report to the Center for Population Research, NICHD-NIH, Bethesda, MD.

Zelnik, M. & Kantner, J. (1980b). Sexual activity, contraceptive use, and pregnancy among metropolitan area teenagers: 1971-1979. *Family Planning Perspectives*, *12*, 230-237.

Zelnik, M. & Kantner, J. (1977). Sexual and contraceptive experience of young married women in the United States, 1966-1971. *Family Planning Perspectives*, *9*(2), 55-73.

Zelnik, M. & Kantner, J. (1980). Sexual activity, contraceptive use, and pregnancy among metropolitan area teenagers: 1971-1979. *Family Planning Perspectives*, *12*, 230-237.

Zelnik, M., Kantner, J., & Ford, K. (1982). *Adolescent pathways to pregnancy*. Beverly Hills: Sage.

Contemporary Sex Roles for Adolescents: New Options or Confusion?

Dianne F. Harrison
R. Clark Pennell

SUMMARY. This article reviews various social influences and their effects on adolescent sex role development, including parents, peers, media, schools, race, social class and religion. The authors conclude that teens may experience sex role strain based on pressures to conform to gender expectations. Implications for social work practice are discussed.

It is now generally agreed that the manner in which we come to acquire our gender or sex roles and identity as female, male, or some position between the two, is determined by a complex interaction of genetic, physiological and sociocultural factors (Money, 1987; Kelly, 1988). During adolescence, the biological and physiological phenomenon of puberty (i.e., the hormonal and other physical bodily changes) interacts with various social and cultural forces (i.e., social class, peer group, parental influences, schools, exposure to the media and so on) to produce a period of physical, social, and emotional development that not only firmly establishes a gender/identity role begun in childhood, but that also moves young people toward adulthood as they learn to become men or women. While the decades of the 1960s and 1970s witnessed a significant lessening of traditional sex role identification, the 1980s have seen a combination of continued changes and new options in sex role

Dianne F. Harrison's teaching and research interests are in the areas of human sexuality, family issues, behavior therapy and practice evaluation.
R. Clark Pennell's interests are in adolescents, and marriage and family interventions.

definitions *and* a reemergence among some individuals of the more traditional forms of masculinity and femininity (Hyde, 1986). For adolescents, these conflicting messages can result in turmoil, fear, confusion, or challenge regarding what is acceptable and desirable for them. Such turmoil and challenge, in turn, can lead to retrenchment (clinging to traditional sex roles), rebellion (shedding of anything traditional), or some combination of the two.

The purpose of this article is to examine the contemporary influences on adolescent sex role development, the various consequences of these influences, and the implications for social work practice on both the micro and macro levels. In this discussion, the terms sex role, gender role, and gender role/identity are used interchangeably to refer to both the private or inner experience of one's self as male or female *and* the outward expression to others of the degree to which one is masculine, feminine, or androgynous (having both masculine and feminine traits).

While the nature versus nurture controversy continues among theorists and researchers investigating the development of sex roles, there is at least some agreement that a significant part of the establishment of masculine and feminine sex roles results from a learning process, i.e., our socialization as male or female (Richmond-Abbott, 1983; Masters, Johnson, & Kolodny, 1988). Disagreement exists over the exact manner in which these roles are learned; i.e., through differential socialization (Kagen, 1976); imitation to achieve self-identity (Kaplan & Sedney, 1980); and/or cultural gender schema (Bem, 1987).

CONTEMPORARY INFLUENCES

As adolescents seek to achieve self-identity, intimacy with others, develop satisfying relationships with peers, and define themselves as sexual beings (Johnson & Alford, 1987), they are exposed to many sources of influence. These sources include family, peer group, schools, religion, media, the racial/ethnic/cultural environment, and current societal expectations regarding masculinity/femininity/androgyny. Obviously, these influences interact to some degree with one another and it is difficult to isolate, for example, the effects of parental influences from those of society, or the media, or the cultural environment. Also, the messages communicated about sex role behavior to adolescents by these sources may vary considerably by region, size of location, social class, and so on. In this section, we will review the major types and content of social influence on today's adolescents, and the extent to which research has demonstrated the consequences of these influences. Unfortunately, much of the research related to sex role development and particularly sex differences in development, is extremely problematic. The area of gender roles is a volatile one; the research literature tends to be methodologically flawed, correlational rather than causal, and full of contradictory findings. Other criticisms have been made relevant to biased research and publication practices (Henley, 1985) and that the majority of samples have been drawn from mostly white middle class populations (Hyde, 1986).

Family

The importance of parental and family influence on sex role development has long been recognized in the literature (Richmond-Abbott, 1983). During adolescence, the family may lose its role as the primary socialization force as teens seek self-identity and independence. However, parents still exert considerable influence through modeling of behaviors, levels of acceptance of their childrens' behaviors, and parental responses to external socialization forces. Research on the effects of child-rearing practices during the adolescent years is scant and what exists is less systematic than the literature on younger children (Ziegler & Dusek, 1985). A couple of studies have found that children were better adjusted when their parents assumed the traditional masculine and feminine roles (Lidz, 1963; Klein & Shulman, 1981). Ziegler and Dusek (1985) reported that teens who perceived their parents as less sex stereotyped were from more emotionally healthy homes. These authors also found that adolescent perception of parental acceptance and restrictiveness was associated with sex roles. Specifically, accepting parents seemed to foster less traditional sex roles (androgyny) in their children while greater parental control was related to more traditional sex roles. This latter finding was especially true for feminine females, who perceived their parents as accepting yet more rigidly enforcing rules and regulations. Ziegler and Dusek suggested that these parenting techniques may in fact foster traditional female sex roles by encouraging dependence and hindering the development of independence (1985).

What about the effects of changing family structures and changing sex role expectations on teenagers? In the current society, a majority of children will spend a part of their lives in single-parent homes, in families where both parents are employed, and/or in families where either the parents, siblings, or the adolescents themselves will assume more androgynous sex roles. Richmond-Abbott (1983) summarized the research on the effects of single-parent families on children's gender identity/role by noting that only a few differences between children in single-parent versus two-parent homes had been found. When differences did exist, the father's absence had typically occurred before the child was age five (most of the research has been done on custodial mothers and absent fathers) and the effects were similar to those found in two-parent households with low father availability. The reported differences in certain areas of cognition (e.g., higher verbal than quantitative scores), self-control (e.g., boys having less control and more antisocial behavior), and some sex-typed behaviors (e.g., "compensatory masculinity" in some boys), may be the result of parental attitudes and behaviors rather than the structure of the home. Richmond-Abbott concluded that, in general, such children do not seem to suffer negative consequences and may in fact be the beneficiaries of more liberal parental sex-role attitudes than is typically found in two-parent homes. A single parent, whether mother or father, is more likely to model androgynous behaviors (perhaps out of necessity) and may expect the same from the children. Also, while some single custodial mothers may be concerned about the lack of a masculine role model for their male children, there is some evidence to suggest that fatherless boys are not entirely lacking in male role models as is often assumed (Herzog & Sudia, 1968). Obviously, there is a need for continued research in this area, particularly longitudinal studies and studies which examine the differential effects, if any, of single parenthood whether by divorce, separation, or death, and sex of custodial parent.

The question of the effects of parental employment on children is plagued by bias as we typically address this issue by examining only the effects of the mother's employment. Few studies have evaluated the effects of the father's work or absence from home because the expectation is that if a parent were to stay at home with the children, it would be the mother. In general, the reported effects of maternal employment on adolescent sex role development have shown either few differences between the children of working and nonworking (i.e., no paid employment) mothers or a more positive effect on girls than on boys. For example, some adolescent daughters of mothers employed outside the home have been found to be more assertive, independent and have more positive career plans of their own (Smith, 1982; Richmond-Abbott, 1983). The mother's attitude toward work, whether satisfied or dissatisfied, also seems to influence the effects on children. Women who are satisfied in their employment may encourage more independence and communicate more positive messages about female work roles (Harrison, Kilpatrick & Vance, 1984; Richmond-Abbott, 1983). However, in the case of two-parent families where both parents have outside paid employment, most children are exposed to conflicting sex role messages. That is, while they may experience female work role models in the home and possibly be encouraged to higher career aspirations, they also witness the mother continuing to bear most of the responsibilities for household tasks and child care (Harrison, 1986). When fathers do participate in household tasks, they tend to be in traditional sex-typed areas such as car repair, yardwork, or garbage disposal (Harrison & Wells, 1988). We can only speculate as to the long term effects of these conflictual nonverbal messages on adolescents when they reach adulthood.

To summarize, parental influence is an important, although no longer primary, source of adolescent sex role socialization. Parental modeling of verbal and nonverbal behaviors, levels of acceptance, and marital and employment status, all may contribute to adolescent gender roles. Most adolescents seem to receive stereotypic sex role messages from their parents, while an increasing number of teens are receiving simultaneous traditional *and* nontraditional sex role messages from parents. Apparently, adolescents who receive primarily nontraditional messages from parents are in the minority. Regardless of which messages parents communicate to their teens related to sex roles, the fact is that parents must compete with other sources of influences, especially the adolescent peer group and the media. For the most part, parents seem to come in third in the competition.

Peer Group

During adolescence, the peer group often replaces the family as the most dominant socialization force, as peer approval may become more important than parental approval (Doyle, 1985). As teens seek their self-identity and learn to develop satisfying relationships with others, they frequently define themselves by their perceptions of how they are viewed by peers (Johnson & Alford, 1987). Particularly in early adolescence, a sense of membership and belonging becomes critical. While the names may vary, almost every high school in the United States has its definite, named peer groups which typically have rigidly defined sex roles (Byer, Shainberg & Jones, 1988). Membership and acceptance by the group are contingent upon conformity to its gender roles with respect to clothing, sexual activities and general life style.

Although peer supported gender roles can vary depending on family, social class and area, there seem to be certain desirable characteristics for males and females which represent typical norms for adolescents in our society. For adolescent boys, such traits include being tough (through body build or athletic achievement), being cool (not showing emotions, not fearful of danger, staying reasonable under stress), being interested in girls and sex, being good at something, being physically attractive, and having an absence of any trait or characteristic that is female or feminine (Abbott-Richmond, 1983; Masters, Johnson & Kolodny, 1988). While there are obvious negative aspects to some of these qualities, the young male who does not fit in or conform is less likely to be accepted or popular and as a result, he may in fact be quite lonely and isolated (Byer, Shainberg & Jones, 1988). For the nonathletic or less physically tough type, he is less likely to be a leader and is more likely to question his masculinity because he has not had access to these culturally defined avenues to masculine identity (Abbott-Richmond, 1983).

For females, the sources of self-identity (and self-esteem) are slightly different. Adolescent girls face tremendous peer pressure to be physically attractive and popular, and in the 1980s, to be achievement-oriented (Masters, Johnson & Kolodny, 1988). These achievements can be in traditional (e.g., cheerleading) or nontraditional female areas (e.g., sports or academics). Pressures related to popularity and achievement can be at odds with one another especially as high achievement may result in a perceived loss of femininity (Schaffer, 1981). Also, the importance that girls place on being pretty and popular (as avenues to femininity and sources of self-identity) is usually stressful because these are qualities over which the individual basically has little control. As definitions of femininity have become more ambiguous (e.g., appropriate dress, career goals, sexual behavior), female adolescents may experience additional stress and confusion. As a result, they may seek their identities through peer approval and peer defined patterns of behavior even more so than males. This possibly excessive desire for approval from others may carry on into adulthood. Although systematic research on this issue is scant, there is some evidence that females who rely on peer relationships to define self and to clarify some of the ambiguity in current feminine sex role norms are more vulnerable in terms of their health and overall well-being (Burke & Weir, 1978).

In general, the peer pressures on male teens relate to qualities that are traditionally masculine and even macho. For females, the sex role norms are more ambiguous and less consistent, incorporating both traditional and nontraditional gender behaviors. For both sexes, there is consequent stress in attempting to conform to these pressures; there may also be conflict between peer and parental messages resulting in further confusion and stress. For the adolescent who does not, or cannot, conform to one or more of the typical peer group norms (this may represent a majority of teenagers), and who also lacks a high degree of self-confidence, supportive and accepting parents, and at least some peer acceptance, we might predict problems in adolescent adjustment and later adult functioning.

Media

Several studies have noted the increased role the media play in the sexual socialization process, a process which includes not only information about sex but also sex role behavior (Darling & Hicks, 1982; Strouse & Fabes, 1985). The influence of the media, especially television, is not surprising, given the fact that some young people spent more time consuming television than in any other activity except sleeping (NIMH, 1982). Unfortunately, heavy viewers are also more likely to think that what is presented on TV represents reality (Strouse & Fabes, 1985). Adolescents tend to watch Music Television (MTV), prime-time programming, soap operas, and commercials; they also consume radio, films, music, and advertisements on any media source. Their consumption of the mass media has been enhanced in this decade by VCRs, Walkmans, "boom boxes," cable TV, and assorted stereo equipment (Strouse & Buerkel-Rothfuss, 1987).

Much of the media content to which teens are exposed depicts sex role stereotypes, distorted and unreliable messages about sexuality, unrealistic images of physical attractiveness, and violence within the context of sexual relationships (Strouse & Fabes, 1985; Byer et al., 1988). Examples of these messages can be found in virtually any day or nighttime soap opera, in currently popular TV programs such as "L.A. Law" and "Cheers," in the majority of the music videos, and in the so-called "teen slasher movies." While there seems to be some trend away from portraying individuals in rigid stereotyped sex roles (Hyde, 1986), the bulk of the popular mass media continues to emphasize, either with subtle or obvious messages: physical beauty (for males and females); physical strength, toughness, and aggressiveness (for males); nonmarital intercourse without contraception or sexually transmitted diseases; and violence, often juxtaposed with sexual themes.

Research on the effects of media on teens has produced some sobering results. For instance, Morgan and Rothschild (1983) found that the amount of television consumption by adolescents was positively associated with traditional sex role stereotypes, particularly for adolescents with low peer affiliation. Adolescents have been shown to use physically attractive media figures as sexual role models (Fabes & Strouse, 1984). Morgan and Gerbner (1982) concluded that television had a negative impact on teenagers' decision to use contraception. In a similar vein, Strouse and Buerkel-Rothfuss (1987) found that the consumption of sexually oriented media, such as soap operas and MTV, may have some influence on sexual permissiveness. When asked about the "pressures to become sexually involved," teenage respondents in one study indicated TV was the greatest source of such pressure; pop music was second (Howard, 1985:273). Adolescent familiarity with popular music has also been associated with greater peer involvement and lesser family involvement (Larson & Kubey, 1983). Finally, Avery (1978) reported that teenagers have developed an increased tolerance for the sex/violence messages on TV.

While direct causal links between the effects of media on adolescent sex roles and sexual behavior have not been firmly established, the existing literature, even with methodological flaws, warrants our attention. At a minimum, it is important to recognize that the media seem to be contributing to the mixed sex role messages given to adolescents and that many of these messages carry severe consequences if they are translated into teenage behavior.

Schools

The educational system in our society serves as a powerful socialization force for our children. In addition to offering a formal curriculum, schools provide instruction in attitudes and values such as cooperation, competition, self-discipline, achievement, and conformity (Byer et al., 1988). On the whole, it also appears that schools still tend to reinforce traditional gender roles, even though explicit differences in terms of the treatment/opportunities given to males and females are becoming rarer (Richmond-Abbott, 1983; Byer et al., 1988). Schools may have subtle means for presenting these messages to adolescents; for example, through the use of sexist textbooks and gender-specific curricula and activities (e.g., cheerleading versus football team).

Teachers are important role models and their own behavior, attitudes, and values, can influence the students' development. If teachers hold traditional sex role expectations and model such behavior in their interactions or if they demonstrate nontraditional attitudes and behaviors, students will tend to conform. High school girls may receive subtle cues from teachers that their abilities are less than male students, especially in areas such as mathematics, and they may be treated rather passively by school guidance counselors unless the girl actively seeks assistance and already has a good idea about her career goals (Richmond-Abbott, 1983).

Another source of gender role stereotyping in the schools is in the sex education curriculum (that is, if one exists). Most school-based sex education programs emphasize the biological and physiological aspects of sexuality, such as anatomy and physiology, reproduction, sexually transmitted diseases, and possibly, contraception (Kenney & Orr, 1984). While this type of information is critical in efforts to reduce the spread of STDs and lessen the incidence of teenage pregnancy, ignoring the psychological, social, and cultural aspects of sexuality may result in, among other things, a "biological determinist view of gender issues" (Whatley, 1987:26). This view would hold that sex hormones are totally responsible for male aggression and sex drive, leading students to conclude erroneously that since these traits are biologically determined males cannot be held accountable for their sexual aggression or sexual urges. For adolescents, the double-standard is reinforced. For example, most of the attention in the "Just Say No to Sex" campaigns has been on the females' responsibility to assertively resist sexual intercourse due to the belief that males are under the control of their "raging hormones" (Whatley, 1987:29).

As in the case of the previously discussed socialization forces, our schools also play an important part in the sex role development of adolescents. In this setting, teens may be given mixed messages regarding gender roles and gender appropriate behavior even though the transmission of traditional sex role expectation appears quite institutionalized.

Race, Social Class, and Religion

As mentioned earlier, the bulk of research on adolescent sex role development has been based on white middle class teens. With respect to race, however, several differences between whites and blacks in expectations for gender role behaviors have been found. (We were unable to locate literature which described differences which may exist for other races.) Many of these differences appear to be based on social class. Smith (1982), for example, noted that black female adolescents in the lower socioeconomic class were faced with the necessity of taking on adult responsibilities (e.g., child care or household tasks) at an earlier age than their white or black middle class counterparts. As a result, they seemed to gain a sense of competency and independence earlier in their development. Black female teens are also more likely to have higher self-esteem, feel more satisfied with their looks, and place less emphasis on popularity than white female teens (Richmond-Abbott, 1983). These more positive traits among black females may be due to family backgrounds where economic need, exposure to female work role models and the relative egalitarian relationships among black men and women create an environment in which the adolescent is aware of alternative options to marriage and reinforced for assertiveness and self-sufficiency (Smith, 1982; Richmond-Abbott, 1983). There is some evidence to indicate that the future plans of black and white female teens to assume both work and parenting roles have become more similar than dissimilar. The motivations for taking on these dual roles, however, appear to be different: for whites, the desire to work may be for self-fulfillment; for blacks, the decisions may be based more on a sense of family economic responsibility (Smith, 1982). At the same time, harsh economic and social realities faced by low income black female teens combined with peer pressures related to sexual activity, lack of sex education, and tolerant attitudes toward teen pregnancy, are more likely to result in higher teen pregnancy rates than for middle class teens. However, the fact that birth rates for unmarried low income white teens have increased significantly in the last two decades lends added support to the position that the problem of teen pregnancy may be more related to economic circumstances and the hopelessness of poverty rather than the stereotypical notion of race being the determinant (Stark, 1986).

For black male adolescents, particularly among the lower class, peer pressures on being tough, cool, and macho may be even greater than among their white middle class counterparts (Richmond-Abbott, 1983). Poor black and white males are likely to engage in more fighting than their middle class peers and, at least among blacks, such fighting may be an attempt to gain status in the black community (Staples, 1978). With respect to athletic achievement, concern has been expressed among some blacks over the exaggerated emphasis placed on black youth for success in sports versus academics, especially in light of the small percentage of athletes who actually succeed in professional sports (Snyder & Spreitzer, 1978).

No single set of experiences characterizes the lives of black male or female adolescents (or their white counterparts); their sex role development is influenced by family background, social class, available role models and the extent to which both mainstream and black cultural values are incorporated (Smith, 1982). In general, however, it appears that black male teens tend to receive highly traditional sex role messages and black females receive some traditional and to a greater extent, nontraditional messages. Many of these trends seem to be based on social class rather than race and hold true for lower class white teens as well.

The role played by religions in the sexual socialization of teens has been controversial. Religions, especially the Judeo-Christian traditions, have been criticized for their historic and current reinforcement of patriarchal power in family and social life (Rush, 1980). Christianity has also been praised by some as the source of a positive ethic of gender equality and sexual pleasure (Gardella, 1987). A significant negative relationship between religiosity and sexual permissiveness for females but not males has been consistently reported in the literature (Strouse & Buerkel-Rothfuss, 1987). These authors speculated that the Judaic-Christian theologies express stronger condemnations of nonmarital sexual behavior for females than males and that for young adults, beginning "sexual activity may be as much a cause of low religiosity as high religiosity is a cause of sexual celibacy" (p. 49). This is another area which deserves further study. The fact that women have not, for the most part, been allowed to serve as priests or rabbis leads us to conclude that religions have been sending fairly traditional messages regarding sex roles to adolescents.

NEW OPTIONS OR CONFUSION?

Thus far we have reviewed various sources and types of social influence on adolescent sex role development in our society. On the whole, it seems that teens, especially females, are receiving conflicting messages about gender behavior from parents, peers, schools, and the media. Male adolescents continue to receive the majority of traditional sex role messages. Some of the effects these influences may have on teens have already been discussed. At this point, we believe that these messages result mainly in confusion and stress and, to a lesser extent, pose new challenges and opportunity. For example, for females new options often mean conflicting expectations (e.g., being sexy and attractive, yet not being sexually active). They also mean they have greater choices in career goals. The new options for females can lead to more freedom and flexibility for males; they can also conflict with traditional male sex role expectations (e.g., male as sexual aggressor and provider). Both young men and women who do not conform to traditional gender role behaviors may find it easier to break through the male or female stereotypes, but they may also be subjected to parent pressure and/or peer ridicule and isolation.

The Sex Role Strain (SRS) paradigm described by Pleck is a useful framework for understanding the confusion/challenge dilemma. This model posits that sex roles are defined largely by societal stereotypes and norms, and they are inherently contradictory, constricting, inconsistent and dysfunctional (Pleck, 1981). Further, the SRS model suggests that these roles are often violated; such violations carry negative social and psychological consequences (more so for males than females). Because of these consequences, most individuals tend to overconform to gender role expectations. Pleck believed that sex role strain is experienced by both males and females and that it has been increased by the historical changes in societal attitudes toward gender behavior.

Is androgynous behavior (presence of both masculine and feminine traits) a solution to this strain? Many authors have suggested that the positive aspects of both masculinity and femininity in an individual can produce advantages such as: higher self-esteem and social competence (Spence & Helmreich, 1978); more flexible behavior patterns (Bem, Martyna & Watson, 1976); and fewer psychological problems (Burchardt & Serbin, 1982). Others have argued that androgyny carries the possibility of negative consequences such as: increased work stress (Rotheram & Weiner, 1983); difficulty in directing behavior effectively (Cook, 1985); and less overall emotional adjustment than masculine males (Jones, Chernovetz & Hanson, 1978). We agree with the observation of Masters, Johnson and Kolodny that ". . . it is too early to know if androgyny is a desirable goal for the future or a potential source of trouble" (1988:288).

It may be that some conflict and sex role strain is inevitable without widespread societal shifts in attitudes and beliefs about sex roles resulting in consistent messages from all sources to teens. In searching for their self-identity, adolescents do have new options available to them, although more so for females than males. Our continued homophobia, especially toward male homosexuals, still exerts considerable pressure on adolescent boys to conform to traditional masculine roles.

IMPLICATIONS FOR PRACTICE

Macro Level

In order to provide new options and increased flexibility for adolescent sex role development without consequent strain and confusion, we recommend that several macro level changes be made. Perhaps most obvious, is the continued need for social workers to lobby for the Equal Rights Amendment that would legally sanction equality between the sexes. Efforts should also be directed toward other legislation related to child care and parental leave policies, for example, that would provide families additional support for maternal employment and the participation of fathers in child rearing.

The social work profession, including our national organizations, should also assume a role in educating the public and the media about the negative messages they perceive in some sexually explicit materials, advertisements, television programming, music videos and films. Given the potentially destructive effects some of these messages have on teens, and our long-standing professional concerns with the exploitation of women and children, it seems only reasonable that we need to educate the public (e.g., via newspaper articles and public service announcements) and influence the media (e.g., via supporting contraception ads on TV and encouraging the hiring of more women in powerful decision-making positions). In line with the SIECUS position, we should not, however, advocate censorship, "insofar as such efforts endanger constitutionally guaranteed freedoms of speech and press" (SIECUS, 1986: 10).

Our attention and energies should further be directed toward state and local policies related to sex education and school curricular content and learning materials. We need to advocate for the inclusion of the social, psychological and cultural aspects of sexuality in addition to the biological aspects in sex education programs (K-12) and the adaptation of sex education curricula for special needs children such as those who have learning, physical and/or mental disabilities. We must also work toward the elimination of sexist classroom materials. School boards, administrators, and teachers need to be informed of not only the overt stereotype messages given to students but the subtle messages as well. Richmond-Abbott (1983) has developed helpful checklists for nonsexist socialization and for classroom teachers that could be used. She also recommends student letter-writing campaigns and reports to administrators, publishers, and community groups to reduce bias.

Micro Level

Our attention on the micro level should be focused on adolescents and their parents. Specifically, teens need to be educated regarding the unrealistic and irresponsible portrayals of males, females and sexual relationships in much of the media. Adolescents can also benefit from training in problem-solving, decision-making, and assertion skills as they relate to sex role behaviors, sexual activity, and peer pressure. Emphasis in counseling and education can be placed on the positive aspects of peer support and tactics for enhancing support systems without eliminating individual choices. An example of the latter would be to assist a teenager in locating a peer system whose values and behaviors more closely matched his/her own (whether in school or outside of school). For both males and females, it would be useful to clarify the new roles available for women and to give permission for an expansion of norms for males. Male adolescents may especially need this permission and education as they are at greater risk for adhering to traditional sex roles (Streitmatter, Santa Cruz & Ellis-Schwabe, 1984). When appropriate in work with both males and females, the social worker should acknowledge the probable sex role strain and direct efforts toward reframing the confusion into "challenge." Lastly, our own modeling of sex role behaviors and attitudes and the behaviors we reinforce or support in the adolescent can also affect positive change.

With respect to parents, we recommend the use of parent training groups as a preventative measure. Such groups are typically popular with parents of adolescents who may not need therapy but yet desire an educational program on the difficulties of coping with teens. Sample topics might include: the effects of the media on teens; the effects of traditional sex role stereotyping; parental modeling; techniques for becoming accepting parents, and parental responses to adolescent peer pressure. Essentially, in addition to education, the strategies employed in this type of group consist of training in communication and problem-solving, anger management and basic techniques of behavior modification. For parents or families who require therapy in situations where sex role development is an issue, the overall intervention strategy we recommend would be quite similar; i.e., education and parenting skills (communication, problem-solving, anger management), as appropriate. We have found that some parents may have just as much difficulty in accepting adolescent sex role behaviors that do not conform to their own as the adolescent may have in developing their self-identity.

CONCLUSION

We have reviewed the various sources of social influence and known effects of these influences on adolescent sex role development. Overall, we suggest that the contemporary gender role development of teens may be characterized primarily by role strain and confusion, yet we believe that ultimately, the new options available for them pose exciting potentials for increased individual freedom and flexibility. Social workers have the opportunity and obligation to turn such confusion to positive challenge by changes at both the macro and micro levels.

REFERENCES

Avery, R.K. (1978, November). Patterns in the life cycle: Adolescents' use of mass media. Paper presented at the Annual Meeting of the Speech Communication Association, Minneapolis, MN.

Bem, S.L. (1987). Masculinity and femininity exist only in the mind of the perceiver. In Reinisch, J.H., Rosenblum, L.A., & Sanders, S.A. (Eds.), *Masculinity/femininity: Basic perspectives* (pp. 304-311). New York: Oxford University.

Bem, S.L., Martyna, W., & Watson, C. (1976). Sex typing and androgyny: Further explorations of the expressive domain. *Journal of Personality and Social Psychology, 34*, 1016-1023.

Burchardt, C.J. & Serbin, L.A. (1982). Psychological androgyny and personality adjustment in college and psychiatric populations. *Sex Roles, 8*, 835-851.

Burke, R. & Weir, T. (1978). Sex differences in adolescent life stress, social support, and well-being. *The Journal of Psychology, 98*, 277-288.

Byer, C.O., Shainberg, L.W., & Jones, K.L. (1988). *Dimensions of human sexuality (2nd Ed.)* Dubuque, IA: Wm. C. Brown Publishers.

Cook, E.P. (1985). *Psychological Androgyny*. New York: Pergamon Press.

Darling, C.J. & Hicks, M. (1982). Parental influence on adolescent sexuality: Implications for parents as educators. *Journal of Youth and Adolescence, 11*, 231-245.

Doyle, J. (1985). *Sex and gender*. Dubuque, IA: Wm. C. Brown Publishers.

Fabes, R.A. & Strouse, J.S. (1984). Youth's perceptions of models of sexuality: Implications for sexuality education. *Journal of Sex Education and Therapy, 10*, 33-37.

Gardella, P. (1986). Christianity has given us a positive ethic of gender equality and sexual pleasure. In Francoeur, R.T. (Ed.), *Taking sides: Clashing views on controversial issues in human sexuality* (pp. 284-292).

Harrison, D.F. (1986, May). Dual-earner families: Current issues in research and practice. Paper presented at the National Association of Social Workers' Conference on Women's Issues, Atlanta, GA.

Harrison, D.F., Kilpatrick, A.C., & Vance, P.V. (1984). Social work practice with dual-career middle class families: Response to a changing family structure. In M. Dinerman (Ed.), *Social work in turbulent world, Selected proceedings of the seventh NASW National Professional Symposium*. Silver Springs, MD: NASW.

Harrison, D.F. & Wells, J.G. (1988). Stress and self-esteem: A comparison of women working outside the home and full time homemakers. Manuscript submitted for publication.

Henley, N.M. (1985). Psychology and gender. *Signs, 2*, 101-119.

Herzog, E. & Sudia, C.E. (1968). Fatherless homes: A review of research. *Children, 15*, 73-81.

Howard, M. (1985). Postponing sexual involvement among adolescents: An alternative approach to prevention of sexually transmitted diseases. *Journal of Adolescent Health Care, 6*, 271-277.

Hyde, J.S. (1986). *Understanding human sexuality*. New York: McGraw Hill.

Johnson, J. & Alford, R. (1987). The adolescent quest for intimacy: Implications for the therapeutic alliance. *Journal of Social Work and Human Sexuality, 5*, 55-66.

Jones, W.H., Chernovetz, M.E., & Hanson, R.O. (1978). The enigma of androgyny: Differential implications for males and females? *Journal of Consulting and Clinical Psychology, 46*, 298-313.

Kagan, J. (1976). Psychology of sex differences. In Beach, F. (Ed.), *Human sexuality in four perspectives* (pp. 87-114). Baltimore: Johns Hopkins University Press.

Kaplan, A. & Sedney, M.A. (1980). *Psychology and sex roles: An androgynous perspective*. Boston: Little, Brown.

Kelly, G.F. (1988). *Sexuality today: The human perspective*. Guilford, CT: The Duskin Publishing Group, Inc.

Kenney, A.M. & Orr, M.T. (1984). Sex education: An overview of current programs, policies and research. *Phi Delta Kappa, 65*, 491-496.

Klein, M. & Shulman, S. (1981). Adolescent masculinity-femininity in relation to parental models of masculinity-femininity and marital adjustment. *Adolescence, 16*, 45-48.

Larson, R. & Kubey, R. (1983). Television and music: Contrasting media in adolescent life. *Youth & Society, 15*, 13-31.

Lidz, T. (1963). *The family and human adaptation*. New York: International Universities Press.

Masters, W.H., Johnson, V.E., & Kolodny, R.C. (1988). *Human sexuality (3rd Ed.)*. Glenview, IL: Scott, Foresman and Co.

Money, J. (1987). Propaedeutics of diecious G-I/R: Theoretical foundations for understanding dimorphic gender identity/role. In Reinisch, J., Rosenblum, L.A., & Sanders, S.A. (Eds.), *Masculinity/femininity: Basic perspectives* (pp. 13-28). New York: Oxford University.

Morgan, M. (1982). Television and adolescents' sex role stereotypes: a longitudinal study. *Journal of Personality and Social Psychology, 43*, 947-955.

Morgan, M. & Gerbner, G. (1982). TV professions and adolescent career choices. In M. Schwarz (Ed.), *TV and teens: Experts look at the issues*. Reading, MA: Addison-Wesley.

Morgan, M. & Rothschild, N. (1983). Impact of the new television technology: Cable TV, peers, and sex role cultivation in the electronic environment. *Youth and society, 15*, 33-50.

National Institute of Mental Health. (1982). *Television and behavior: Ten years of scientific progress and implications for the eighties* (DHHS Publication No. DM 82-1195). Washington, DC: U.S. Government Printing Office.

Pleck, J. (1981). *The myth of masculinity*. Cambridge, MA: MIT Press.

Richmond-Abbott, M. (1983). *Masculine and feminine – Sex roles over the life cycle*. Reading, MA: Addison-Wesley Publishing Co.
Rotheram, M.J. & Weiner, N. (1983). Androgyny, stress, and satisfaction. *Sex Roles, 9*, 151-158.
Rush, F. (1980). *The best kept secret*. Englewood Cliffs, NJ: Prentice-Hall.
Schaffer, K. (1981). *Sex roles and human behavior*. Cambridge, MA: Winthrop.
Sex Information and Education Council of the United States (1986). *SIECUS Report, 14*, p. 10.
Smith, E.J. (1982). The black female adolescent: A review of the educational, career and psychological literature. *Psychology of Women Quarterly, 6*, 261-288.
Snyder, E. & Spreitzer, E. (1978). *Social aspects of sport*. Englewood Cliffs, NJ: Prentice-Hall.
Spence, J.T. & Helmreich, R.L. (1978). *Masculinity and femininity: Their psychological dimensions, correlates, and antecedents*. Austin, TX: University of Texas Press.
Staples, R. (1978). Masculinity and race: The dual dilemma of black men. *Journal of Social Issues, 34*, 173.
Stark, E. (1986). Young, innocent, and pregnant. *Psychology Today*, Oct., 28-30, 32-35.
Streitmatter, J.L., Santa Cruz, R.M., & Ellis-Schwabe, M. (1984). Early adolescent attitudes toward sex roles. *Journal of Early Adolescence, 4*, 231-238.
Strouse, J. & Fabes, R.A. (1985). Formal vs. informal sources of sex education: Competing forces in the sexual socialization of adolescents. *Adolescence, 20*, 251-263.

Acquaintance Rape Among Adolescents: Identifying Risk Groups and Intervention Strategies

Andrea Parrot

SUMMARY. This article integrates the findings of a number of works which address acquaintance rape in adolescent and young adult populations. Social workers can be most helpful by empowering the victim or assailant through counseling to change the patterns which contributed to the rape, and may also serve in an advocacy role with schools, police, the medical community, family, and friends.

INTRODUCTION

Acquaintance rape (forced sexual intercourse between people who know each other) most often happens between the ages of fifteen and twenty-five. This article will discuss the phenomenon of acquaintance rape in a variety of dimensions: its frequency, patterns of occurrence, characteristics of potential assailants, and behaviors that place adolescents at risk of becoming acquaintance rape victims. In addition, attention is given to the counseling needs of victims as well as appropriate advocacy roles for the social worker to adopt with schools, police, medical professionals, and the victim's family and friends.

Although most of the research on acquaintance rape has been conducted on late adolescents (18-20 year olds) and young adults, younger adolescents are also at risk and have been studied to a

---

Andrea Parrot's research interests focus on acquaintance rape in high risk populations. Her most recent book is titled *Coping With Date Rape and Acquaintance Rape*.

limited extent. Acquaintance rape often happens during the dating years to young women and men, usually to those who have trouble with social relationships. Approximately 20% of college women report forced sex victimization during college or *before* (Parrot, 1985; Koss, 1985); although Koss, Gidycz, and Wisniewski (1987) suggest that females in the general population probably experience a higher rate of acquaintance rape than do college women. This suggests that perhaps more than 20% of late adolescents who do not go to college may be acquaintance rape victims.

Social workers are often able to recognize behaviors that signal possible sexual abuse: a negative change in social relationships, a drop in grades, withdrawal, or a change in sexual behavior (Finkelhor, 1984; Burgess & Holstrom, 1979). Yet, because the phenomenon of acquaintance rape has received so little attention in the professional literature, the social worker may neglect to inquire about this specific form of abuse when working with an adolescent.

There are special characteristics that acquaintance rape victims share which make them especially vulnerable to that experience. However, once they have become victims, they are not likely to define what has happened to them as rape because they often feel guilty and think they have been responsible in some way. Therefore, the challenge professionals face is to identify those who have been victims, and help them deal with the victimization; identify those who are potential victims and help them avoid an acquaintance rape; and to identify those who may commit acquaintance rapes to prevent them from becoming assailants.

Adolescents who refuse to talk about sex, or talk about it all the time, especially if this behavior pattern is unusual for them, may have been victims of acquaintance rape. Acting out sexually, or withdrawing from relationships with friends may also be signals of acquaintance rape involvement. They often blame other victims for their rapes which may lead to social isolation. Changes in relationships with family or friends may signal victimization.

Any of these things can be signs of acquaintance rape victimization. Past victims need help, but so do those who are at risk of future victimization. Both groups need intervention to prevent future victimization or to help them heal emotionally. Adolescents need special attention because they do not yet have the life experience or maturity which may help them avoid acquaintance rape or sexual assault.

Acquaintance rape is not a new phenomenon, however, it has been recently identified and is receiving increasing coverage. Kanin described acquaintance rape in the scholarly literature in 1957, but then instead of occurring on the first or second date as it may today, the rape was likely to occur later in the relationship.

Today more victims are willing to talk about their rapes than in the past since the women's movement has created an environment in which females feel justified in being angry about violence against them. In addition, we only recently have terms to describe crimes like date and marital rape. Many members of society have been sensitized about these issues. Some may think that the increased sensitivity is more widespread than it actually is. Consequently, some young women may think that they are not at risk by asking men out or going back to a man's apartment after a date. The women's movement may have been responsible for increased female assertiveness, and increased male acceptance of female assertiveness. But not all males accept or condone this change. Some men think that if a female asks a male out on a date, she is "loose," and is "asking for sex." So the increased assertiveness and freedom a female enjoys now may put her at increased risk for acquaintance rape, especially if her partner still thinks traditionally. Since most acquaintance rape victims are female, this article will focus on heterosexual rape of female victims.

LITERATURE REVIEW

Very little acquaintance rape research has been conducted using early adolescent subjects. Most research on acquaintance rape has been conducted using the college student and young adult acquaintance rape population. Issues related to older populations may be similar to those regarding acquaintance rape among younger adolescents.

Some people feel that in particular situations forced sex is permissible. Males' assumptions about their right to sex was studied at

Texas A & M and Indiana University; 106 college students were asked to respond anonymously regarding acceptability of behaviors in dating situations. In this study, almost all of the males felt that it was acceptable for a female to ask a male out. They felt that he should accept the invitation (Muehlenhard & McFall, 1981); but indicated that in such a situation the man might view the female as very promiscuous.

The subjects were given three descriptions of heterosexual dating interactions, which varied with respect to who initiated the date, where the couple went, and who paid. They were then asked if there were any circumstances in which forced or coerced sex was justified. Many males rated intercourse against the female's wishes as significantly more justifiable when asked out by a female, when the male paid, and when the couple went to the male's apartment (Muehlenhard & McFall, 1981).

UCLA researchers asked similar questions of a group of teens (Giarruso, Johnson, Goodchilds, & Zellman, 1979). A large percentage (54%) of adolescent males studied felt that forced sex was acceptable if the young woman said "yes" even though she later changed her mind. What if the young woman was saying "yes" to kissing, but "no" to intercourse? If she is not very specific about what she is saying "yes" to, the man may interpret the "yes" to imply that sexual intercourse is acceptable (Parrot, 1987).

Almost 40% of males in the UCLA study felt that forced sex was acceptable if a male spent a lot of money on a female. Over one third of the males interviewed in the UCLA study believed that forced sex is acceptable if a male is so turned on that he thinks he can not stop. This is a widely held misconception about male sexuality which is often used as an excuse to force sex. In fact, there is no time in the male sexual response cycle when a male actually can not stop, except immediately before ejaculation (Masters & Johnson, 1966).

Some high school females in the UCLA study also felt that it is acceptable for a male to force a female to have sex. Almost one third of the females in the study thought that forced sex was acceptable if they had dated a long time (32%), if she says she is going to have sex with him and then changes her mind (31%), if she let him touch her about the waist (28%), and if she "led him on" (27%)

(Giarruso et al., 1979). From these findings it is clear that females, too, need to reconsider justification for rape.

Kikuchi reported in a 1988 study of 1700 Rhode Island sixth through ninth graders that 50% of the respondents felt that a woman was asking to be raped if she walks alone at night and dresses seductively. When asked if a female's previous sexual experience justified forced sex, 31% of the males and 32% of the females responded affirmatively.

Of students in seventh through ninth grade in the Rhode Island study 24% of the males and 6% of the females said that a man has a right to force sex on his date if he spends money on her. Two thirds of the seventh through ninth grade males and half of the seventh through ninth grade females said that the male has a right to force sex if a couple had been dating for more than six months.

These attitudes develop at a very early age. Families, schools, peers and media all contribute to boys' and girls' developing attitudes condoning acquaintance rape.

TEENAGE SEXUAL BEHAVIORS

Preventing acquaintance rape is extremely difficult because many adolescents think that males should initiate sex and females should act coy. Adolescents frequently "play sexual games" in which neither partner is clear about his or her intentions. Some may move along a behavioral continuum from mutual exploration to acquaintance rape without seeing major differences in these expressions. An explanation of each stage follows Table 1.

TABLE 1

Teenage Sexual Experiences Continuum

1	2	3	4	5	6	7
Mutual sexual explora-tion	Per-suasion of a reluctant partner	Exploita-tive sexual activity	Sexual coercion	Sexual harass-ment	Acquain-tance rape	Stranger rape

(Adapted from Bateman and Stringer, 1984.)

1. *Mutual sexual exploration* is a common teenage activity. Through this activity teens learn about initiating sexual activity, touching, and mutual pleasure giving. This behavior is an important element of normal teenage psycho-sexual development.
2. *Persuasion of a reluctant partner* also is a common teenage behavior. Most often, the male is the one persuading the female to comply, but not always. Persuasion can be acceptable if the reluctant partner is treated with respect, and his or her feelings are taken into account.
3. *Exploitative sexual activity* happens when one person "uses" the other to get what he or she wants sexually. For example, he may agree to go steady with her if she will have sex with him, even though he does not intend to actually go steady with her. Girls may also exploit their partners by being manipulative.
4. *Coercion* is a situation in which one person threatens harm if the reluctant partner does not agree. For example, he may threaten to make her get out of the car in the middle of winter when they are "parking," and she will have to find her own way home if she does not comply with his wishes.
5. In *sexual harassment* situations the victim is violated in some interpersonal and sexual way without being given a choice. For example, he may pat her buttocks as she passes him, or he may stare at her breasts in a way that makes her uncomfortable.
6. *Acquaintance rape* is forced sex against the victim's will and without consent, by an offender known to the victim; a friend, date, teacher, employer, etc. If the victim complies because of fear for life or safety, or has sex when mentally incapacitated (asleep, or passed out), that is acquaintance rape. Force or violence are *not* necessary. The victim may even have had sex with the offender voluntarily before.
7. *Stranger rape* is a situation in which the victim has been forced to have intercourse by a stranger, and often violence is used to get the victim to comply. Many stranger rape victims report thinking that they are not going to get out of the situa-

tion alive. In some states men may legally be considered victims.

IDENTIFYING ADOLESCENTS AT RISK

There are certain characteristics which victims of date and acquaintance rape often possess. Although many victims will exhibit these characteristics, some young people will become victims who are very different from the type of person described here. For example, most victims of acquaintance rape are females, but some males also become victims. The F.B.I. estimates that 10% of sexual assaults are committed against males (F.B.I., 1984). In addition, some females who do not fit the profile at all may be caught in the wrong place at the wrong time and are raped by people they know as a result.

Most acquaintance rape victims are female. They often have low self-esteem, external locus of control (when they think the events that take place in their lives are beyond their control), exhibit traditional sex role behavior patterns (females are not assertive and play "games" on dates; males act "macho") (Koss, 1985), have experienced past victimization (Tsai, Feldman-Summers & Edgar, 1979), and want to have a higher status within the peer group. These females may not achieve their maximum capability academically, because if they do well in school they are worried that they will not be asked on many dates. These adolescent females may believe that males do not want to date females who excel over males.

The best way for these young women to raise their status, in their opinions, is to affiliate themselves with high status males. High status males are often athletes, or fraternity men. The female may think that once she is the girlfriend of a man in the "in group" she will be an accepted member of the "in group" too. Even if he is exploiting her she may be so worried about losing her newly found status, that she will not tell her date that she does not like what he is doing to her. She may not interpret warning signs correctly which may indicate that he is a dangerous person to be dating. For example, he may ignore her repeated requests to stop rubbing her buttock while dancing.

Although the offenders of most female victims are male, this is not always the case. Female victims may be forced sexually by other women, but this is rare. Males may become victims of either male or female assailants. Regardless of the gender of the attacker, a male victim is not likely to report the assault because he will probably be embarrassed, ashamed, concerned about what this means about his masculinity, feel that he should have been able to defend himself, and be confused about his gender orientation (Benedict, 1985).

IDENTIFYING POTENTIAL ASSAILANTS

Many men who force sex on their dates do not know that what they have done is wrong (Parrot, 1986). They may think that any sexual encounter gives them a right, under certain circumstances, to sex. Men may also believe that a woman never really means no in a sexual situation. These men are likely to have low self-esteem, prior experiences as victims of degradation and humiliation, traditionally masculine sex role stereotypic behavior patterns (acting "macho"), to exhibit other forms of anti-social behavior (such as driving drunk), and a desire to raise their status within the peer group. Neil Malamuth (1981) studied 42 college men regarding their proclivity to rape, and about 35% of the men studied indicated that they would be likely to rape if they could be assured of not being caught. Although many men may be in situations which could lead to acquaintance rape, only about 5% reported actually committing acquaintance rape (Koss et al., 1987).

PATTERNS IN ACQUAINTANCE RAPE

Groth (1979), while studying rapists, identified a three stage pattern in rapists' behavior during acquaintance rapes. Although this is a general acquaintance rape pattern, all victims and rapists are different. First, a rapist engages in intimate behaviors which make a female feel uncomfortable (for instance, by putting his hand on her thigh, or kissing her in a public place after knowing her for only a short time). This is common in party and bar situations when the music is so loud that the couple must be very close to each other to hear. In such situations it is not possible to maintain a comfortable distance from others.

If the victim does not clearly object, the rapist proceeds to the second stage in which he desensitizes the victim to the intrusion by escalating the behavior (moving his hand to her buttocks, for example). She may feel increasingly uneasy as a result of this behavior, and suggest going outside for "fresh air" hoping that she can create physical distance from him. Unless she actually tells him that she is uncomfortable with his "roaming hands," he may misinterpret her suggestion as meaning she wants to be alone with him. The third stage occurs when they are in an isolated place (such as outside, in his apartment, in his car, etc.) and the rapist insists on intercourse.

COUNSELING ACQUAINTANCE RAPE VICTIMS

Many victims of acquaintance rape will be difficult to identify because they may not call what happened to them "rape." Victims may feel guilty or responsible for causing the rape. They may believe that rape happens when a stranger jumps out of the bushes and brutally attacks a woman. Because her experience is different than that described above, she may not know how to define what happened to her. She may say "I got myself in a bad situation," or "He took advantage of me," rather than calling it rape. Male victims may not believe that men can be raped, or are so humiliated that they will not report their rape to anyone. Therefore the social worker faces a difficult challenge in identifying acquaintance rape victims.

Typical Dysfunctional Patterns of Victims

Most victims who do not seek help exhibit dysfunctional behavior patterns. Burkhart (1983) identified three of the most typical patterns:

She may exhibit *non-discriminating sexual behavior patterns* (sex with many members of the other sex). If she was a virgin and believed that virginity is good and non-virginity is bad, she may think she is now bad and has no legitimate reason to refuse sex to anyone if she can not use virginity as an excuse.

She may *withdraw from social interactions* because she does not feel she can trust her judgement. When she did trust her judgement, she chose a rapist to date. Therefore, she feels her judgement is faulty. Consequently, she stops making decisions which rely on her judgement, and withdraws.

She may *repress* the rape memory in a desire to get back to normal. As a result she may exhibit occasional emotional explosions when she is under stress and reminded of the rape. This reaction may be triggered by something as innocuous as a male touching her shoulder in the same way the rapist did. The reaction to the recollection of the rape usually precipitates recurring crises.

Implications for Social Work Practice

In acquaintance rape as with most crimes, the unfounded report rate to the police is extremely low. Therefore if a female claims to have been raped, she probably was. She runs the risk of losing friends and family if she does report, and is likely to gain nothing by reporting. This is because most people believe the rape myths. If people allowed themselves to believe that acquaintance rape is possible, they would have to face their own increased vulnerability. Therefore, most people do not believe acquaintance rape victims.

The reaction of the first person the victim tells usually determines how the victim feels about herself, and how she will proceed. If a young woman seeks out a social worker and confides that she has been a victim of acquaintance rape, she needs guidance. Therapists should believe the victim, should act as if they do, or refer the victim to someone who can be more helpful. Local rape crisis centers can be a source of educational information and therapeutic consultation for social workers wishing to learn more about the dynamics involved in acquaintance rape and its aftermath.

For a social worker to be helpful he or she must learn the facts about acquaintance rape. It is also important for the social worker to know the rape law in his or her state. The law is not important so that the victim may press charges, but to let her know that what happened really was rape (Parrot, 1988).

The victim is likely to feel out of control. The rapist took control away from the victim by raping, and others around the victim may be contributing to the feelings of lack of control by blaming, not believing, or not respecting the victim's wishes. The victim needs to regain a sense of control, and needs to feel believed about the rape. The social worker can help the victim select those people who give credence to the attack and who will be supportive. Likewise, the victim will need to reduce contact with those who are disbelieving or who blame her, at least until she is stronger emotionally.

It is best to reduce the amount of guilt the victim feels for any dysfunctional decisions made during the rape (such as getting drunk), and instead to emphasize helping the victim think about how to handle a similar future situation for the best outcome. She needs to be empowered by learning how to avoid an acquaintance rape, so that if she gets into a similar situation in the future, she will know some effective strategies to get out of the situation.

The decision to report the event to the police should be her own. She needs to make her own decisions to feel in control of her life again. The social worker can be most helpful by informing the victim as completely as possible what the outcomes of each option will be, and supporting the victim in her decision.

Helping Victims to Select Options

The victims of acquaintance rape may feel that the social worker is one of the few people with whom she can share information and feelings. In addition to helping the adolescent assess how she can identify supportive peers and family members, the social worker can also be an advocate by providing information and support if the victim decides to report the assault to local authorities. The victim may choose to tell no one, a few who are close to her, therapists, school authorities, and/or the police. The decision of whom to tell and how to proceed legally lies with the victim alone.

Telling friends. The victim should only tell those who will be supportive, and who will not insist on a specific course of action. If friends are pressuring the adolescent to do something uncomfortable, the social worker may be most helpful by helping her find ways to stop seeing those friends.

Telling families. The victim may need help and support to do this because families often blame the victim, and therefore are not good resources for the victim. Families may need counseling support. Some family members feel like victims too; others may want to kill the rapist; all experience emotional trauma about the rape.

Reporting to the authorities at school. This is important if the victim wants the assailant punished or removed from the institution. High schools must respond according to their *Disciplinary Code Book*, which usually requires contacting an appropriate social service agency (such as the Department of Social Services or the Rape Crisis Center), and reporting to the police if the rape occurred on school grounds. In addition they may suspend the assailant, transfer him, notify his parents, and provide the support of a guidance counselor, social worker or psychologist. Colleges may expel, suspend, require community service, move the assailant's residence, put him on probation, or rescind recognition of a fraternity which condoned or encouraged the rape.

If school authorities believe rape myths they are not likely to be supportive to the victim. They may not know the proper protocol to deal with acquaintance rape situations. The victim should be prepared for this possibility. The social worker can serve as an advocate by informing school authorities of the law, the school's options and responsibilities. The social worker may also help teachers, counselors and administrators determine the best course of action for the victim, and make sure these procedures are carried out.

Reporting to the police for information (only). The information about the rape may be kept on file to determine a pattern if this assailant is a repeat offender. The victim will not have to press charges if she reports for information only, but will be more readily believed if she chooses to press charges later.

Suing in civil court. If the victim does not think she can win in criminal court, she may sue in civil court for a financial award for pain and suffering, and expenses for therapy and medical care. The victim may sue the assailant, or a third party, such as a landlord who did not provide a safe environment. The victim has a better chance of winning a civil case than a criminal case.

Reporting to the police to press charges. Most acquaintance rapes do not result in conviction in the criminal courts, but if the victim has a strong case and wants to press charges, she should be supported. A strong case is one in which she has had medical evidence collected, she has bruises, she did not go to the assailant's room or invite the assailant to hers, she had not been drinking (etc.). Although these conditions are not necessary for forced sex to be a crime, a jury is more likely to convict if these elements are present.

Most cases of acquaintance rape that are tried in criminal court do not result in conviction. In fact, if the assailant is found guilty the conviction is usually overturned on an appeal (Estrich, 1987). Judith Rowland, an Assistant District Attorney in San Diego was successful in obtaining convictions by introducing expert testimony to establish the presence of the rape trauma syndrome in acquaintance rape cases (Rowland, 1984).

CONCLUSION

Acquaintance rape of adolescents is an especially difficult problem because many teenagers do not identify what has happened to them as rape. Therefore, they are not likely to seek help immediately. A social worker may happen upon information about an acquaintance rape or may have to draw out the information. By the time an adolescent talks with a social worker about an acquaintance rape she has probably been blamed by others for "asking for it," and probably has also blamed him or herself. Victims need education about acquaintance rape and how to avoid future victimization.

Social workers can be most helpful on this issue through individual counseling of the victim or assailant after the rape, or by empowering those at risk with prevention strategies. Often, working on improving self-esteem is one of the best prevention strategies a social worker can employ. The victim may also need help in deciding whom to select as support people, and how to tell them. In addition, family members may need counseling to help them cope with their feelings about the victim and the rape. They may need help determining how to be most helpful to the victim.

Social workers may also be helpful in an advocacy role with the school, police, the medical community, friends, and family. Members of all of those groups may need education to better understand acquaintance rape to help them deal with a current victim. However, social workers can also be effective in providing education to community groups so that they will understand acquaintance rape better. Education may be one of the most important strategies to empower adolescents to be able to avoid acquaintance rape.

REFERENCES

Adams, C., Fay, J. & Loreen-Martin, J. (1984). *No Is Not Enough: Helping Teenagers Avoid Sexual Assault*. San Luis Obispo, CA: Impact Publishers.

Bateman, P. & Stunger, G. (1984). *Where Do I Start? A Parents' Guide for Talking to Teens about Acquaintance Rape*. Teen Acquaintance Rape: A Community Response Project. Seattle, WA.

Benedict, H. (1985). *Recovery–How to survive sexual assault for women, men, teenagers, their friends and families*. Garden City, NY: Doubleday & Company, Inc.

Brownmiller, S. (1975). *Against our will: Men, women, and rape*. New York: Simon & Schuster.

Burgess, A.N. & Holstrom, L. (1979). Sexual disruption and recovery. *American Journal of Orthopsychiatry*, *49*, 648-657.

Burkhart, B. (1983, November). Acquaintance rape on college campuses. A paper presented at the Rape Prevention on College Campuses Conference in Louisville, Kentucky.

Estrich, S. (1987). *Real rape*. Cambridge: Harvard University Press.

F.B.I. (Federal Bureau of Investigation) (1984). *Uniform crime reports*. Washington, DC: U.S. Government Printing Office.

Finkelhor, D. (1984). *Child Sexual Abuse*. New York: The Free Press.

Finkelhor, D. & Yllo, K. (1985). *License to rape, sexual abuse of wives*. New York: The Free Press.

Groth, N. (1979). *Men who rape: the psychology of the offenders*. New York: Plenum Press.

Giarrusso, R., Johnson, P., Goodchilds, J. & Zellman, G. (1979). Adolescent cues and signals: sexual assault. Paper presented to a symposium of the Western Psychological Association Meeting, San Diego, CA.

Kanin, E. (1957). Male aggression in dating-courtship relations. *American Journal of Sociology*, *63*, 197-204.

Kikuchi, J.J. (1988, April). What do adolescents know and think about sexual abuse. A paper presented at the National Symposium on Child Victimization, Anaheim, CA.

Koss, M. (1985). The hidden rape victim: Personality, attitudinal and situational characteristics. *Psychology of Women Quarterly*, *9*, 193-212.

Koss, M.P., Gidycz, C.A. & Wisniewski, N. (1987). The scope of rape: Incidence and prevalence of sexual aggression and victimization in a national sample of higher education students. *Journal of Consulting and Clinical Psychology*, *55*, 162-170.

Malamuth, N. (1981). Rape proclivity among males. *Journal of Social Issues*, *37*, 138-157.
Masters, W. & Johnson, V. (1966). *Human Sexual Response*. Boston: Little Brown.
Muehlenhard, C. & McFall, R. (1981). Dating initiation from a woman's perspective. *Behavior Therapy*, *12*.
Parrot, A. (1985). Comparison of acquaintance rape patterns among college students in a large co-ed university and a small women's college. A paper presented at the 1985 National Society for the Scientific Study of Sex Convention, San Diego, CA.
Parrot, A. (1988). *Coping with date rape and acquaintance rape*. New York: Rosen Publishing Group.
Parrot, A. (1986). Emotional Impact of Acquaintance Rape on College Women. A paper presented at the Midcontinent Region Convention of the Society for the Scientific Study of Sex, Madison, WI.
Parrot, A. (1987). *Facilitators Manual for STOP DATE RAPE!* Cornell University: Ithaca, NY.
Polonko, K., Parcell, S. & Teachman, J. (1986, November). A methodological note on sexual aggression. A paper presented at the National Society for the Scientific Study of Sex Convention, St. Louis, MO.
Rowland, J. (1985). *The ultimate violation*. New York: Doubleday & Company.
Russell, D.E.H. (1982). *Rape in marriage*. New York: McMillan Publishing Company.
Tsai, M., Feldman-Summers, S. & Edgar, H. (1979). Childhood Molestation: variables related to differential impacts on psychosexual functioning in adult women. *Journal of Abnormal Psychology*, *88*, 407-417.

Preventing HIV Infection Among Black and Hispanic Adolescents

Steven P. Schinke
Gary W. Holden
Michael S. Moncher

SUMMARY. Acquired immune deficiency syndrome (AIDS) has no known cure. Due to its irreversible course, AIDS frequently ends in death. Consequently, preventive interventions with adolescents offer promise for combatting AIDS in America. This article focuses on the reasons for and nature of such interventions with the high-risk groups of Americans: Black and Hispanic Americans. The article reviews the nature of AIDS among Black and Hispanic Americans. Next, the advantages of a preventive intervention approach to AIDS are noted. The article concludes with a discussion of the promise and limitations of interventions for AIDS prevention among the target populations of American adolescents.

Human immunodeficiency virus (HIV) infection is a prodrome of acquired immune deficiency syndrome (AIDS). In a short time, AIDS and HIV infection have captured considerable scientific attention. Much of that attention has focused on biomedical issues, including the discovery and testing of drugs to treat AIDS or to inoculate people against HIV infection. Less attention has been given to interventions for reducing HIV infection risks through in-

---

Currently the three authors are executing and planning applied research studies on the prevention of health related problems among ethnic-racial minority and majority culture adolescents.

Research reported in this article was supported in part by the National Institute on Drug Abuse (DA05356, DA03277), and the National Cancer Institute (CA29640, CA44903).

Address reprint requests to: Steven P. Schinke, Columbia University School of Social Work, 622 West 113th Street, New York, NY 10025.

travenous drug use and unsafe sexual activity. Particularly neglected are interventions for preventing HIV infection among Black and Hispanic Americans. This paper addresses the incidence and prevention of AIDS among Black and Hispanic American adolescents.

AIDS AMONG BLACK AND HISPANIC AMERICANS

Presently in this country, Black Americans are 25% of all adult AIDS cases and 58% of all pediatric AIDS cases (Morgan & Curran, 1986). Hispanic Americans are 15% and 22% of all adult and pediatric AIDS cases in the United States. To put these figures in perspective, Black and Hispanic Americans are approximately 12% and 6% of the country's population. Among pediatric AIDS cases, Black children have an incidence of 15.1 times the white incidence. Hispanic children with AIDS show a cumulative incidence of 9.1 times the incidence for white children. As for heterosexually transmitted AIDS, one-half of all such cases are Black and one-quarter are Hispanic (Morbidity and Mortality Weekly Report [MMWR], 1986). Black and Hispanic women currently account for 51% and 21% of all female AIDS cases in the United States.

As such, Black women have a cumulative incidence of AIDS 13.1 times the incidence for white women. The cumulative incidence of AIDS for Hispanic women is 11.1 times the incidence for white women. By 1991 the Centers for Disease Control (CDC) expects a five-fold increase in the numbers of Black and Hispanic Americans with AIDS.

RISK FACTORS

HIV infection is commonly transmitted by intravenous (IV) drug use and sexual activities. By intravenously injecting drugs, users of heroin and other substances contract and transmit HIV through dirty and shared needles, syringes, and related paraphernalia. The Centers for Disease Control of the United States Public Health Center in Atlanta reports the ethnic-racial distribution of AIDS cases attributable to IV drug use as follows:

> AIDS patients who are IV drug abusers are predominately black (51%) or Hispanic (30%). Children with AIDS whose parents abuse IV drugs are also predominately black (51%) or Hispanic (30%). (MMWR, 1986, p. 663)

In New York City, one-third of all AIDS patients to date have injected drugs (Drucker, 1986; Frank, Hopkins, & Lipton, 1986). The number of IV drug related AIDS cases in the city rose 253% in the last 3 years. "The common element in the transmission of AIDS to children and heterosexuals," according to the city's Commissioner of Health, "is intravenous drug use" (Joseph, 1986, p. 22).

Most IV drug users in greater New York City are Black and Hispanic. In a survey of drug treatment facilities, Black and Hispanic adults accounted for 68% of all patients in the City and 59% of all patients in Newark (National Institute on Drug Abuse, 1982). Another study of the City's drug treatment agencies found HIV antibodies in 42% of all Black patients, 42% of all Hispanic patients, and 14% of nonminority patients (Schoenbaum, Selwyn & Klein, 1986).

Data from the Schoenbaum et al. (1986) study also showed nonminority patients to be twice as likely to use clean IV needles when injecting drugs as were Black and Hispanic patients. After controlling for needle sharing, other research found that Black and Hispanic drug users had higher rates of HIV seroprevalence than nonminority drug users (Chaisson, Moss, Onishi, Osmond, & Carlson, 1987). Further, surveys of military recruits and blood donors similarly note more HIV seropositivity among ethnic-racial minority Americans than among majority culture Americans (Peterson & Bakeman, in press; Ward, Grindon, Feorino, Schable, & Allen, 1986).

Such findings led the AIDS Program Coordinator of the Centers for Disease Control to write,

> Drug abuse and acquired immunodeficiency syndrome (AIDS) are two of the most critical public health problems receiving justified public attention in the United States . . . IV drug abusers in the rest of the nation may not have HIV infection

> rates as high as those in the Northeast, but the potential for further spread is obvious. (Drotman, 1987, p. 143)

Sexual transmission of HIV is a risk for the partners of IV drug users, gay and bisexual men, and persons with multiple partners (Eckholm, 1985; Devita, Hellman, & Rosenberg, 1985; McKusick, Horstman, & Coates, 1985; Polk, Fox, Brookmeyer, Kanchanaraksa, Kaslow, Visscher, Rinaldo, & Phair, 1987). In the past year, heterosexually transmitted AIDS cases for New York City increased 112%. HIV transmission through heterosexual contact is disproportionately frequent among Black and Hispanic adults. Of all women with AIDS who had bisexual partners, 35% are Black and 14% are Hispanic (MMWR, 1986). More striking are prevalence rates of 48% and 38% for Black and Hispanic adults with AIDS who were the heterosexual partners of IV drug users.

PREVENTIVE INTERVENTION

Due to its irreversibility, AIDS is better prevented than treated. Risk factors associated with HIV infection are in fact preventable. Intravenous drug use and unsafe sexual practices lend themselves to preventive intervention. Increasingly, policy makers note the promise of preventing AIDS, as illustrated by the U.S. Surgeon General, Everett Koop. Among other sources, Dr. Koop's position on AIDS was reported by the Consortium of Social Science Associations (1986):

> U.S. Surgeon General Dr. C. Everett Koop gave one of the most remarkable public statements of recent times promoting behavioral and social science when he spoke to the nation on the control of the spread of the AIDS virus. Koop's statement . . . to the President made it clear that for the foreseeable future the most effective policy for responding to the AIDS crisis is direct intervention at the group and family level aimed at specific target groups and aimed at promoting specific behaviors and discouraging others. (p. 1)

Because this advocacy of interventions to prevent AIDS marks a policy shift, the Surgeon General's remarks deserve scrutiny. In his statement to the President, Dr. Koop said,

> Many people, especially our youth, are not receiving information that is vital to their future health and well-being. . . . Education about AIDS should start at an early age so that children can grow up knowing the behaviors to avoid to protect themselves from the AIDS virus. AIDS is not spread by casual, nonsexual contact. It is spread by high-risk sexual and drug-related behaviors—behaviors that we can choose to avoid. (1986, p. A24)

Further to Dr. Koop's report, President Reagan was quoted as saying, "Despite intensive research efforts, prevention is the only effective AIDS control strategy" ("Reagan Adopts AIDS Education Rules," 1987, p. 1). Buttressing these calls for preventive approaches to reduce the risks of HIV infection, are conclusions from a study by the Institute of Medicine (IOM) and the National Academy of Sciences (NAS). Based on their data, Drs. Baltimore and Wolff (1986), the directors of that study wrote:

> We are convinced [that] significant heterosexual spread of the AIDS virus is occurring now in the U.S. We concluded that it will become an increasingly larger proportion of AIDS cases if we don't act immediately to educate the general public, especially those with multiple sexual partners, about how to protect themselves. We are particularly concerned about sexually active adolescents. (p. 30)

Likewise, the CDC called for interventions to prevent AIDS. Concluding a Morbidity and Mortality Weekly Report on AIDS among Black and Hispanic Americans, the CDC wrote:

> Until an effective therapy or vaccine is available, prevention of HTLV-III/LAV infection depends on education and behavioral modification of persons at increased risk. . . . Programs to prevent transmission of HTLV-III/LAV infection through

> heterosexual contact and perinatal exposure also need to consider that approximately 75% of heterosexual patients, 73% of women with AIDS, and 92% of children with perinatally acquired infection are black or Hispanic." (MMWR, 1986, p. 666)

But as the CDC also observed, "Education and prevention programs may be less effective in reaching minority populations unless specifically designed for those groups" (MMWR, 1986, p. 666).

Theory based, culturally sound, and empirically tested interventions are needed to prevent AIDS among Black and Hispanic Americans. Effective and efficient interventions, moreover, will involve adolescents because of their ability to permanently benefit from strategies aimed to prevent HIV infection and AIDS and, concurrently, to promote adaptive and healthy social functioning (cf. Fullilove, 1988). Toward developing interventions to prevent HIV infection and to promote social competence among Black and Hispanic adolescents, the remaining sections of this article lay a theoretical foundation for culturally sensitive and age-relevant strategies.

THEORETICAL FOUNDATION

Theory to support intervention strategies for preventing HIV infection among Black and Hispanic American adolescents reflects concepts of cultural orientation, social learning, and support networks.

Cultural Orientation

As a theoretical concept to guide interventions for preventing HIV infection, cultural orientation is perhaps more salient for Hispanic American youth than for Black American youth. Relative to their Black American peers, Hispanic American adolescents often are recent immigrants to this country. Hispanic youth born in America, moreover, are apt to have parents and other close relatives who were born outside of the United States. Consequently, many Hispanic adolescents and young adults are exposed to two cultures:

their origin or home Hispanic culture and their host or new U.S. culture.

By virtue of being exposed to two or more cultures, some Hispanic youth may experience conflicts or confusion regarding their cultural orientation. Research findings shed empirical light on the possible influence of cultural orientation in respect to adaptive and maladaptive behavior among American Hispanic youths. In her study of Puerto Rican American youth, Palleja (1986) learned that adolescents who aligned themselves equally with Hispanic and non-Hispanic cultures were at less risk for problem behavior than youth aligned exclusively with one or the other culture. Others have discovered similar relationships between acculturation and behavior disorders among Hispanic and non-Hispanic samples (Szapocznik, Scopetta & King, 1978). These findings imply that effective interventions to prevent HIV infection among Hispanic adolescents will help youths view themselves biculturally, as fully enfranchised members of Hispanic and American cultures.

Cultural orientation concepts applicable to Black American youth are less clearly defined due to a longer time period from initial entry to U.S. society and due to an infinitely more complex struggle for equality in America. Still, parallels exist between the bicultural orientation of Black and Hispanic Americans. Black adolescents may well profit from preventive interventions that help them put into proper context and perspective their dual and possibly compatible orientations as representing two cultures. Interventions to prevent HIV infection and AIDS and to promote social competence among Black and Hispanic adolescents, therefore, should recognize and incorporate theoretical concepts of cultural orientation respective to each target ethnic-racial population.

Social Learning

Social learning theory regarding cognitive and behavioral skills can also guide interventions for preventing HIV infection and AIDS risks among Black and Hispanic youth. Potentially beneficial strategies to increase youths' cognitive problem-solving skills come from our past interventions to help adolescents avoid drug use and risky sexual activity (Schinke, Schilling, & Gilchrist, 1986; Schinke, Zayas, Schilling, & Palleja, in press).

Through cognitive coping strategies, preventive intervention can also help Black and Hispanic adolescents instruct and reward themselves for steps toward decreasing their risk of HIV infection. Intervention strategies to enhance youths' behavioral skills can include interpersonal communication skills. Combined, cognitive and behavioral intervention strategies derived from social learning theory will have an increased likelihood of effecting positive change among Black and Hispanic adolescents relative to HIV infection, AIDS, and health promoting behavior.

Support Networks

Support networks are potent forces in the lives of Black and Hispanic Americans. Still, support networks are underresearched as a means to build, strengthen, and sustain Black and Hispanic adolescents' prevention efforts. By tapping these networks, preventive intervention strategies can show family and kinship members how they can reinforce youths' efforts to reduce HIV infection risks. Such intervention could also encourage family and kinship members to develop additional supports to help youths avoid HIV infection risks from drug use and unsafe sexual activity.

Together with skills based elements, social network enhancement strategies may not only increase Black and Hispanic adolescents' personal competence related to HIV infection prevention, but also synergistically serve to quicken youths' rate of learning. Over time, a combined and synergistically effective intervention program may additionally help adolescents' maintain and generalize their learning and apply it to novel and high-risk situations related to HIV infection, AIDS, and other problem behaviors.

DISCUSSION

Besides their implications for preventing AIDS, the sociocultural strategies and concepts described in this article offer a framework for understanding multiple influences that affect HIV infection risk among American Black and Hispanic adolescents. Cultural orientation factors, social learning, and support networks are among influences important to the developmental tasks facing all youth. To prevent HIV infection, interventions with Black and Hispanic youths must take into account developmental forces encountered by all American adolescents and influences specific to Black and Hispanic Americans.

Caveats are in order about the generality of concepts and sociocultural strategies advanced here. Black Americans and Hispanic Americans are diverse populations. Black and Hispanic Americans are more heterogenous than homogenous populations relative to socioeconomic and many variables; language differences further separate groups of Hispanic Americans.

Lending further caution to guidelines for preventing AIDS are the vagaries of adolescence. Depending on their gender, development, and life-style, Black and Hispanic adolescents may respond differently to interventions for preventing intravenous drug use and unsafe sexual practices. These caveats notwithstanding, theoretical concepts and prevention strategies put forth here provide a foundation for interventions to prevent HIV infection among Black and Hispanic adolescents. What is more, these concepts and the strategies they suggest hold promise not only for reducing risks of AIDS, but also for preventing other psychosocial problems with drugs, sexuality, and interpersonal behavior among Black and Hispanic adolescents. Perhaps this discussion of AIDS risks and sociocultural prevention strategies will encourage more intervention research to lower the likelihood of HIV infection among young Black and Hispanic Americans.

REFERENCES

Baltimore, D., & Wolff, S. M. (1986). *Confronting AIDS: Directions for public health, health care, and research*. New York: National Academy Press.

Chaisson, R. E., Moss, A. R., Onishi, R., Osmond, D., & Carlson, J. R. (1987). Human immunodeficiency virus infection in heterosexual intravenous drug users in San Francisco. *American Journal of Public Health*, 77, 169-171.

Devita, V., Hellman, S., & Rosenberg, S. (1985). *AIDS: Etiology, diagnosis, treatment, and prevention*. New York: Lippincott.

Dr. Koop's Decent AIDS Dissent. (1986, October). *The New York Times*, 26.

Drotman, D. P. (1987). Now is the time to prevent AIDS. *American Journal of Public Health*, *772*, 13 and 143.

Drucker, E. (1986). AIDS and addiction in New York City. *American Journal of Drug and Alcohol Abuse*, *12(1 & 2)*, 165-181.

Eckholm, E. (1985, October 28). Women and AIDS: Assessing the risks. *New York Times*, C-1.

Frank, B., Hopkins, W., & Lipton, D. S. (1986). Current drug use trends in New York City, June 1986 (Research report). New York: New York State Division of Substance Abuse Services.

Fullilove, R. E. (1988). Minorities and AIDS: A review of recent publications. *Multicultural Inquiry and Research on AIDS*, *2(1)*, 3-5.

Joseph, S. (1987, January). Research on AIDS. *The New York Times*, 24.

Morbidity and Mortality Weekly Report. (1986). *Acquired Immunodeficiency Syndrome (AIDS) among Blacks and Hispanics United States*, *35(42)*, 655-666.

McKusick, L., Horstman, W., & Coates, T. J. (1985). AIDS and sexual behavior reported by gay men in San Francisco. *American Journal of Public Health*, *75*, 493-496.

Morgan, W. M., & Curran, J. W. (1986). Acquired Immunodeficiency Syndrome: Current and future trends. *Public Health Reports*, *101*, 459-465.

National Institute on Drug Abuse. (1982). National drug abuse treatment utilization survey. *Statistical Series F*, No. 10.

National Institute of Mental Health. (1986). *Coping with AIDS: Psychological and social considerations in helping people with HTLV-III Infection*. (DHHS Publication No. ADM 85-1432). Washington, DC: U.S. Government Printing Office.

Palleja, J. (1986). The impact of acculturation on the behavior of second-generation Puerto Rican adolescents. Manuscript submitted for publication.

Peterson, J., & Bakeman, R. (in press). AIDS and IV drug use among ethnic minorities. *Journal of Drug Issues*.

Polk, B. F., Fox, R., Brookmeyer, R., Kanchanaraksa, S., Kaslow, R., Visscher, B., Rinaldo, C., & Phair, J. (1987). Predictors of the acquired immunodeficiency syndrome developing in a cohort of seropositive homosexual men. *The New England Journal of Medicine*, *316(2)*, 61-66.

Reagan Adopts AIDS Education Rules. (1987, February 23). *Medicine & Health*, 41(8).

Schinke, S. P., Schilling, R. F., & Gilchrist, L. D. (1986). Hispanic and Black adolescents, prevention, and health promotion. *Behavioral Medicine Abstracts*, *7*, 109-114.

Schinke, S. P., Zayas, L. H., Schilling, R. F., & Palleja, J. (in press). Hispanic adolescents, unplanned pregnancy, and preventive intervention. *Practice Applications*. St. Louis, MO: Center for Adolescent Mental Health, Washington University.

Schoenbaum, E. E., Selwyn, P. A., & Klein, R. S. (1986). Prevalence of and risk factors associated with HTLV-III/LAV antibodies among intravenous drug abusers in methadone programs in New York City. Paper presented at the International Conference on AIDS, Paris, France.

Szapocznik, J., Scopetta, M., & King, O. (1978). Theory and practice in matching treatment to the special characteristics and problems of Cuban immigrants. *Journal of Community Psychology*, *6*, 112-122.

Ward, J. W., Grindon, A. J., Feorino, P. M., Schable, C. A., & Allen, J. R. (1986). Epidemiologic evaluation of blood donors positive on the anti-HTLV-III/LAV enzyme immunoassay (EIA). Paper presented at the International Conference on AIDS, Paris, France.

Social Service Needs of Lesbian and Gay Adolescents: Telling It Their Way

Lucy R. Mercier
Raymond M. Berger

SUMMARY. Lesbian and gay adolescents begin to explore their social and sexual identities in environments which are generally unfavorable to the development of positive self-esteem. Little is known about how these adolescents face this challenge. This survey of lesbian and gay adolescents explores the nature and extent of their psychosocial problems and the persons and resources to whom they turned for help. Social service needs centered on the issues of identity management, depression, limited resources for getting help, and getting along with family members.

Fear and misunderstanding about homosexuality pervade our society (Berger, 1987; DeCrescenzo, 1983/1984; Paul, 1982). Negative social attitudes toward individuals who identify themselves as homosexual increase the likelihood of rejection and misunderstanding by family, friends and social service providers who could otherwise serve as valuable supports for these women and men. Lesbians and gay men who are beginning to explore and accept their sexual-

---

Lucy R. Mercier is a clinical social worker with the outreach and prevention program of Tri-City Mental Authority in Pomona, CA. In addition to her clinical work with children and families, Ms. Mercier trains caregivers on effective suicide intervention with youths.

The author of *Gay and Gray: The Older Homosexual Man* (University of Illinois Press, 1982; Alyson, 1984), Dr. Berger has published widely in the areas of lesbian and gay concerns, aging, and evaluation of social work practice.

This research report was made possible by a grant from California State University, Long Beach.

ity may experience ostracism and ignorance just at a time when they need social support in order to develop a healthy integration of social and self-concepts. In particular, lesbian and gay youth, long an invisible part of American culture, represent a high-risk population for social, psychological and health concerns (Hippler, 1986).

This study was designed to explore the special problems and concerns of adolescents who identify themselves as lesbian or gay. The purposes of this study were to determine the range and type of psychosocial problems experienced by lesbian and gay adolescents, and to assess the personal and social support services used by adolescents to address these problems.

NEEDS AND RESOURCES

Social pressures, developmental tasks, and lack of resources combine to create a unique reality for adolescents who are lesbian or gay. According to experts who work with lesbian and gay adolescents (e.g., Hippler, 1986; Vergara, 1983/1984), depression is one effect of the social problems encountered by these youth and attempted suicide is a common result. Hippler (1986) reported that "homosexual youths are six times more likely to attempt suicide than are heterosexual youths" (p. 44).

Problems at home are also a reality for many lesbian and gay adolescents. Gibson (1982) reported that gay youth who participated in her short term residential program were more likely than heterosexual youth to be physically abused at home and more likely to attempt suicide. They also dropped out of school more often because of peer harassment. Hippler (1986) interviewed directors of lesbian and gay youth social service agencies, who agreed that gay adolescents are over-represented in the runaway population and, without help, many end up on big city streets.

Substance abuse is another major problem for lesbian and gay youth and adults alike. Fifeld (1975) estimated that 31 percent of lesbians and gay men in Los Angeles County showed signs of alcoholism or problem drinking, a rate three times higher than that for non-gay adults. Fifeld's research design may have over-represented the problem, but further evidence suggests that members of the lesbian and gay community are more likely than others to experience chemical dependencies. For example, a recent study conducted in Orange County, California, concluded that "the incidence of drug and alcohol abuse among gays is about double that among heterosexuals" (United Way of Orange County, 1986, p. 146).

The many problems of heterosexual adolescents are addressed by helping professionals who specialize in this area, and by special programs such as teen pregnancy prevention, substance abuse and suicide counseling. However, little or no attention is given to the unique circumstances of the adolescent with a lesbian or gay identity. Where service providers recognize the homosexual potential of many adolescents, they often intervene to punish and suppress the development of a gay identity, a type of service which is harmful, rather than beneficial for the adolescent (e.g., Wasserman, 1976).

A recent Health Planning Council report summarized the situation:

> Not all agencies and professionals are able or disposed to deal sympathetically with sex-role or sexual-identity conflicts; many may continue to confuse different sexual *orientation* with role/identity *conflict*. There is a need for a network of social support services and mental health resources which will accept persons with different sexual orientation and provide services appropriate to the problem each person wishes to resolve. Moreover, service agencies and professionals must be acceptable to clients if services are to be effective. (Orange County Health Planning Council, 1984, p. 244)

DEVELOPMENT OF A LESBIAN OR GAY IDENTITY

Lesbian and gay adolescents are in a developmental stage characterized by the search for identity and the struggle for individuation. With puberty comes the beginning of sexual maturity and often, the awakening of sexual feelings and impulses which mark the beginning of the process of self identification as lesbian or gay.

Moses and Hawkins (1982) described the process of coming out as "one of the most difficult and potentially traumatic experiences a gay person undertakes" (p. 80). The stages of coming out include signification (coming out to self) and coming out to others. Concerns about psychological health, safety in the non-gay world, and role confusion, are common in the coming out process, and lesbian and gay individuals often seek help from professionals, friends, or family members during this time.

Coming out as lesbian or gay involves social and psychological risk-taking. The fear of the unknown is an initial hazard. Individuals who are able to overcome this obstacle may then encounter "society's most deadly weapons": silence (lack of role models and unavailability of lesbian/gay history), lies (distorted media presentation), isolation (lack of readily available support systems), intimidation (from ridicule to threats of loss of rights) and physical violence (street attacks, rape) (Baetz, 1984; Bohn, 1983/1984). The lesbian and gay press is filled with personal anecdotes and descriptions of situations in which these weapons are used against lesbian and gay individuals. Recently, the special problems of coming out in adolescence have been addressed in books such as *One Teenager In Ten* (Heron, 1983) and *Young, Gay and Proud* (Alyson, 1983).

In-depth studies on the development of a healthy lesbian or gay identity suggest that an individual undergoes a complex process of integration, stabilization and synthesis of ideas and information on self and sexuality. Lewis (1984) cited feelings of difference in early childhood as the beginning of a process of identity formation for lesbians. Vague ideas of "not fitting in" may emerge during childhood; later the adolescent may experience withdrawal and isolation. As homosexual feelings emerge, dissonance between social and self-concepts begins to arise. This period of turmoil may be followed by a grieving process which takes the woman through a time of denial and bargaining before acceptance of homosexuality and identification with the lesbian community is achieved. Experimentation in relationships, the search for community, and reestablishment of severed family ties may typify the woman's attempts to integrate her lesbian identity with her social reality. Following emergence of a stable lesbian identity, a continuing process of integration and adjustment is established by which the woman can assert a positive self-concept. Clinicians' roles in this model of coming out include education and advocacy, as information and support are needed in the development of a healthy lesbian identity.

Berger's (1983) model of homosexual identity formation delineated more specifically the process characteristic of self identification as lesbian or gay. A state of identity confusion, resulting from dissonance between overt and covert behaviors and self-image, precedes the entire process and acts as a catalyst for changes in self-image for those who later identify themselves as homosexuals. Self-labeling and association with peers are first steps in establishing a new homosexual identity, while the task of "identity management" is an ongoing dilemma as these individuals choose between completely covert identity, selective disclosures of sexual orientation, or aggressive/militant identification as lesbian or gay. Self-acceptance is a final, ongoing phase, and involves a synthesis of behaviors and self-image. This model of identity formation suggests that self identification as lesbian or gay is independent of sexual experience and labelling by others, but that these factors often occur simultaneously with the conflict and struggle of identity formation. The importance of environmental factors in this complicated and arduous set of tasks is evidenced by suggestions for clinicians to assist clients with identity management and peer association as these subtasks are "prerequisites of self acceptance" (Berger, 1983, p. 134).

SPECIAL ISSUES OF LESBIAN AND GAY YOUTH

Although no studies specifically examine the experiences of individuals who deal with the developmental tasks of adolescence concurrently with homosexual identity formation, Vergara (1983/1984) suggests that these combined stresses are linked with "increased isolation, insecurity and acting out behavior" (p. 23). More specific accounts of homosexuality in youth have referred to the particularly traumatic effects of teasing by peers, negative reactions of parents and teachers and intense feelings of self-hatred which accompany this period (e.g., Heron, 1983).

Moses and Hawkins (1982) suggested that individuals who come out in adolescence usually have been exposed to a great deal of negative information about homosexuality. As a result, young people hesitate to discuss their feelings with others in order to avoid ridicule and punishment. At the time, such isolation restricts supportive interactions and access to information about lesbian and gay resources. Vergara (1983/1984) discusses the negative effects of "invisibility" in young gays and lesbians as "helping professionals continue to perpetuate the myth that young men and women cannot be sure of their sexual preference" (p. 23). As a result, in spite of the intense pain fostered by the experience of lesbian and gay youth, many are reticent to approach potentially helpful adult acquaintances, parents or human service professionals. "Although self chosen peer contacts may seem safe, knowledge by adults carries the threat of labeling and exposure beyond the boundaries desired by the young person" (Woodman & Lenna, 1980, p. 87).

Woodman and Lenna (1980) suggested that, while the heterosexual adolescent is encouraged to explore her or his sexuality during adolescence, lesbian and gay youth frequently discover only loneliness and fear. When young lesbians and gays come out as homosexual they often experience a series of insults to their self-esteem as well as interference with developmental tasks. For example, their families may respond with overt or covert homophobia in the form of hostility, ridicule or denial, or the adolescent's "sense of self" may be denied as parents attempt to stop or change the youth's sexual or affectional behavior.

Relationships with peers may also present difficulties. Adolescents who disclose homosexual feelings to peers are often exploited or threatened with unwanted disclosure to others, while adolescents who completely hide homosexual feelings face unrealistic expectations for heterosexual behavior. Their silence also increases social isolation and reinforces the already negative beliefs these youngsters have about themselves.

Moses and Hawkins (1982) summarized many of the unique problems of lesbian and gay adolescents:

> In general, a large part of the problem that adolescents face in coming out can be attributed to their status as minors. They have no mobility, poor access to information, no rights in the matter of sexual preference; and they are also surrounded by peers who are struggling with their own sexuality and enmeshed in the super-conformist and highly antigay world of adolescence. Being minors, they cannot be actively helped by

> adult gays, which means that one of the major sources of support for gays is not available to them. (p. 82)

The lesbian and gay community itself is beginning to recognize the problems and strengths of these adolescents. Hippler (1986) reported that the problems of today's youth are similar to the issues faced by lesbians and gays in the 1960s. Naming isolation, family problems, and violence as major obstacles confronting adolescents, Hippler outlined various ways in which communities have responded to this group's needs. From the handful of model programs available to youth around the country, the conclusion was drawn that resources are neither accessible nor broad enough in scope to accommodate all the needs of lesbian and gay youth.

METHOD

A questionnaire was developed to gather information about the respondents' general concerns and problems, as well as their concerns about use of lesbian and gay resources. The participants were also asked to indicate individuals whom they had approached for help with a personal concern, and to rate how helpful they believed that parents, counselors, teachers, friends and others would be in assisting them with a problem. Additional items specified the age, gender, living situation and sexual orientation of respondents, as well as the degree to which others were aware of their sexual orientation. Several of the questions contained open-ended response items which were designed to encourage respondents to provide additional information about resources used and problems experienced. In addition, one item requested respondents to describe any negative consequences they had experienced as a result of seeking help from another individual.

The questionnaire was pre-tested through distribution to a small sample of lesbian and gay respondents. Feedback from the pre-test group was used to modify ambiguities and formatting problems. In addition, respondents' comments resulted in the addition of some items to the lists of resources used and problems experienced.

For purposes of this study the authors defined adolescents as individuals from thirteen to 21 years of age. This is consistent with commonly accepted definitions of adolescence in the social science literature (e.g., Garrison & Garrison, 1975; Manaster, 1977).

All respondents were recruited from Orange County, California. Orange County consists of a group of communities located about 30 miles southeast of Los Angeles. The area is generally affluent and politically conservative, and is characterized by a suburban lifestyle with high geographic dispersion and reliance on automobile transportation (Orange County Board of Supervisors, 1985). Unlike neighboring Los Angeles County, Orange County is not rich with human rights and social service organizations run by the lesbian and gay communities, although a few such resources exist.

Given a population of 682,104 young women and men between thirteen and 21 years of age in Orange County, the authors estimate the size of the lesbian and gay adolescent population to be 54,570 (Orange County Administrative Offices, 1982). This is based upon the assumption that approximately eight percent of the population is primarily lesbian or gay (Berger, 1982b).

The senior author contacted six groups: three youth "rap" groups (two of these were sponsored by a Gay and Lesbian Community Service Center and one by a Youth Outreach Service; two groups were for both sexes and one served lesbians only); two lesbian and gay student unions at local colleges, and a support group for young people sponsored by Parents and Friends of Lesbians and Gays. The senior author attended one meeting of each group.

At these meetings she described the study as a needs assessment of lesbian and gay youth, assured respondents of anonymity, and explained the informed consent form and instructions for answering the questionnaire. Respondents were asked to return their completed questionnaires directly to the senior author; stamped and self-addressed envelopes were also given to respondents who had taken additional questionnaires to be completed by friends not in attendance at the meetings. A total of 80 questionnaires were distributed in this manner.

Data were coded onto a computer file and Crunch Interactive Statistical Package (CRISP) was used to analyze the material (CRUNCH Software, 1984).

RESULTS

Of the 80 questionnaires distributed to six community groups, 49 usable questionnaires were returned, for a return rate of 61 percent. Seventy-three percent of returned questionnaires were from the three rap groups. Five were returned by mail.

Lesbians were under-represented in this sample: only 30 percent of respondents were female. Age of respondents is summarized in Table 1. Since no 13- or 14-year olds responded, ages ranged from 15 to 21, with a mean age of 19 years. Older adolescents predominated: 83 percent were 18 years of age or older.

Consistent with other surveys of homosexuals drawn from community sources, not all respondents said they were exclusively homosexual (Bell & Weinberg, 1978). Two-thirds of respondents described themselves as "entirely lesbian/gay," one-fourth as "mostly lesbian/gay, partly heterosexual" and the remainder as "equally lesbian/gay and heterosexual." No respondents described themselves as "mostly" or "entirely heterosexual."

Seventy-one percent of respondents lived with parents or other relatives, while the remainder lived with a gay or non-gay roommate or with a same-sex lover. No respondents lived alone or with a lover or spouse of the opposite sex.

Table 1

Age of Respondents

Age	%
15	2
16	8
17	6
18	16
19	22
20	27
21	18

Note. N = 49. No respondents were 13 or 14 years old.

It might be suspected that adolescent homosexuals are more likely to "pass" than adult homosexuals (that is, be known as heterosexual by others), since they may not yet be certain of their sexual orientation, and they are most likely to conceal their identity in response to peer pressure. This group of adolescents however, was known as homosexual to a surprisingly large number of people, particularly family members.

Table 2 indicates that the great majority of these adolescents were known as lesbian or gay to their parents, to brothers and sisters, and to counselors. While gay friends almost always knew of the respondent's sexual orientation, the data suggest that these adolescents were selective about which of their non-gay friends were told or

Table 2

Others' Awareness of Respondents' Lesbian or Gay Identity

Person	N[1]	Knows	Suspects	Neither Knows Nor Suspects
Mother	47	70	15	15
Father	42	60	7	33
Closest friend	49	82	10	8
Counselor or therapist	23	76	0	16
Employer	32	31	34	34
		All Know	Some Know	None Know
Sister(s)	33	58	15	27
Brother(s)	37	51	3	46
Lesbian/Gay friends	47	96	4	0
Non-gay friends	48	31	52	17
Teachers	44	5	45	50
Co-workers	37	19	43	38

[1] Respondents who checked "does not apply" or "don't have any" were not included in the analysis for that item. All individuals responded to the "Father" and "closest friend" item; two individuals did not respond to the "Brothers" item; one individual did not respond to each of the remaining items.

made aware. Employers, teachers and co-workers were less likely to know.

Although this sample is too small to draw a definitive conclusion, mothers and sisters were more likely than fathers and brothers to be aware of or to suspect respondents' homosexuality. If this trend is real, it is consistent with anecdotal evidence from the authors' work with adolescents which suggests that they confide more readily in female rather than male family members and friends. This is not surprising, since males tend to be more homophobic than females (Price, 1982).

Psychosocial Problems

In response to a list of problems and concerns, these adolescents were asked to check those problems which they had encountered in the last year. They could also name "other" problems which were not listed, or indicate they had not had any problems (Table 3). Only two of the 49 respondents reported no problems within the last year. The most common problems, those experienced by over half of respondents, were: telling others you are lesbian or gay, depression, being misunderstood, dating and getting along with your family. Substantial minorities had difficulty meeting and getting along with others, resolving religious questions, being harassed by peers and doing well in school. Only a handful reported problems with alcohol, drugs, suicide or the law.

Although this study did not directly measure the severity of psychosocial problems, the authors did tabulate the number of problems cited by each adolescent. These ranged from zero to ten, out of a total of fourteen possible problems. Most respondents (60 percent) reported having between three and six problems within the last year.

Seeking Help

Where do lesbian and gay adolescents turn for advice and guidance? Respondents were presented with a list of persons or groups and asked to check all resources to which they had turned for advice or guidance in the past year (Table 4). Friends were an almost universal resource, used by a higher percentage of respondents (90

Table 3

Report of Problems Experienced in the Past 12 Months (N= 49)

Problem	%
Telling others that you are lesbian or gay	61
Depression	59
Being misunderstood	55
Dating	55
Getting along with your family	53
Meeting other lesbian or gay people	41
Getting along with others/making friends	35
Resolving questions concerning religion	27
Teasing, threats or violence from peers	22
Grades/teachers/other school problems	22
Alcohol or drugs	12
Attempting suicide	8
The police/getting arrested	4
Other	12
None	4

Note: "Other" problems listed were: Maintaining relationships, suicide of a lover, dealing with an ex-lover, the work place, and finding help for concerns about coming out.

percent) than any other resource. Since these adolescents were recruited primarily from lesbian/gay groups, it is not surprising that over half had sought help from these groups. Still, this finding documents the importance of these groups to adolescents who think of themselves as lesbian or gay.

Almost half of respondents in this study had turned to a parent or to a girl/boyfriend. Relatively few of these adolescents sought help from siblings or from adults from the larger, presumably heterosexual world outside the family: counselors, therapists, teachers and other school personnel.

Even fewer called upon services provided by the lesbian/gay community itself, especially where the service was not targeted spe-

Table 4

Resources Consulted in Past Twelve Months for Advice or Guidance (N = 49)

Resource	%
Friends	90
Lesbian or gay support group for youth	57
Parents	45
Lover/girlfriend/boyfriend	45
Sisters/brothers	29
Counselor/therapist (mental health professional)	27
Teacher	20
School counselor	10
Support groups for families of lesbians/gays	10
Religious counselor	8
Coach/youth group leader	8
Other lesbian or gay resources	8
Gay and lesbian community center hotline	6
Non-gay support group	2
Other non-gay resources	0

Note: Respondents were asked to choose as many of the above as applied. Therefore, percentages total more than 100.

cifically for younger persons: family support groups, gay "hotlines" and other lesbian and gay community services. This finding suggests that lesbian and gay adolescents often do not find the help they need, even in areas where the homosexual community has a service network in place. These services may simply not meet the needs of gay adolescents if they are focused solely on adults, and do not reach out to the adolescent community.

When these young people had a problem or concern they generally consulted more than one resource. Almost three-quarters (71 percent) reported that they had spoken to at least three or four resources in the past year. A quarter had consulted at least five to six resources. This was a group of young people who understandably had many problems and concerns, and they made the effort to seek guidance for these concerns.

Sometimes the search for informed and useful guidance is a difficult one for the adolescent. Even where help is provided by lesbian and gay services in the adolescent's community, there are a number of barriers which may prevent or discourage the young person from getting that help. Analysis of responses showed that two-thirds had at least one concern that would make them reluctant to use a gay and lesbian agency or service. Table 5 summarizes these concerns. About a fifth of respondents had concerns about concealing their homosexuality: they might be seen in a lesbian/gay setting or a family member might discover their homosexuality. From these data it is clear that, while 60 to 70 percent of these adolescents are "out" to their parents, most of the remaining youngsters are quite fearful that their parents will "find out."

Even though these adolescents were recruited primarily through a lesbian/gay group, a fifth reported that they generally did not know where to find such groups. A fifth also reported that lack of transportation was a barrier to using a lesbian/gay service. In suburban areas like Orange County, with poor public transportation, this is a serious impediment to use of services, particularly since many support groups meet in the evenings when public transportation is least available. The present study may actually under-represent the mag-

Table 5

Concerns About Use of Lesbian and Gay Community Resources (N = 32)

Concern	%
Don't have transportation	20
Afraid of being seen entering/leaving a lesbian/gay function	20
Don't know where groups for young lesbians/gay are	20
Afraid parents or other family members will find out	18
Services are offered at inconvenient times	14
Can't afford it	10
Don't have the kinds of programs I want	8
Afraid someone will make a pass at me	4
Other	6

nitude of this problem, since the sample is skewed in favor of older adolescents who generally have access to cars. Younger adolescents were less likely to be in attendance at meetings in which respondents were recruited.

Adolescents are sometimes discouraged from visiting lesbian/gay resources because they have adopted the pervasive mythology that gays are child molesters. Apparently this sample of adolescents was sufficiently sophisticated to discount this concern: only two were afraid that someone might "make a pass" at them.

Getting the Help They Need

Seeking help is one thing. Getting help that is useful and also shows respect for the individual's dignity is far from assured for the lesbian or gay adolescent. In this study, adolescents rated how helpful they thought fourteen different resources would be in assisting with a personal concern. Their responses are summarized in Table 6.

Friends again emerged as the most helpful resource; almost all respondents believed that friends would be helpful. This, no doubt, accounts for the observation that adolescents turn most often to their friends for help (Table 4). Lesbian and gay youth groups were also perceived as helpful by the great majority of these adolescents.

Very few respondents had actually turned to "other" (non-adolescent) lesbian and gay support groups or agencies (Table 4). However, two-thirds reported that they believed these groups *would* be helpful. This suggests that barriers such as inadequate transportation and lack of information may impede adolescents' use of these groups.

With the exception of "counselor/therapist," most respondents believed that religious counselors, school counselors, teachers, coaches and other "helpers" from the larger heterosexual world were likely to be unhelpful or they were uncertain about their helpfulness. While parents and therapists were believed to be helpful by many, there is clearly an overwhelming preference for reliance on friends and people met through a lesbian/gay youth group.

Homophobia has been defined as an irrational negative emotional reaction to homosexuality and to homosexuals (Weinberg, 1972; Gramick, 1983). Because homophobia is so widespread in our cul-

Table 6

Perceived Helpfulness of Resources (Percentages)

Resource	N	Helpful/ Very Helpful	Not Sure	Unhelpful/ Very Unhelpful
Friends	48	90	6	4
Lesbian/gay youth group	47	87	11	2
Other lesbian/gay resources	46	65	35	0
Support group for families of lesbian/gays	44	64	34	2
Counselor/therapist	46	63	24	14
Lesbian/gay hotline	46	57	37	6
Parents	49	47	18	35
Coaches/youth group leaders	45	42	40	10
Teachers	46	30	43	27
School counselor	46	15	41	43
Non-gay support group	44	11	50	39
Religious counselor	45	9	31	60
Other non-gay resources	44	7	73	20

ture, adolescents are often uncertain about whom they can trust. Many adult lesbian and gay men have reported negative experiences, when as adolescents they confided in a peer or an adult (Berger, 1982). These negative experiences can play a decisive role in the individual's subsequent adjustment, if the individual adopts the same homophobic feelings that were communicated by a trusted and respected "helper." They may also diminish the individual's future willingness to seek help or to self-disclose.

Thirty-five percent or 17 out of 49 adolescents in this study reported that they had turned to someone for help and had a "bad experience." For over half (59 percent) or these respondents, the other person was a friend. Seven adolescents had a bad experience with family members or helping professionals. It appears that peers are the most frequently used and most helpful resource; but having turned to their peers most often, this is the group that is also most likely to be the source of the bad experiences which are reported by a minority of adolescents.

DISCUSSION

Given negative social attitudes about homosexuality and the need for many lesbians and gays to conceal their orientation, truly representative samples of this population are not available (Paul, 1982). Respondents were recruited for this study through lesbian and gay organizations and social networks. Adolescents who had not sought help from an organization and those who had no lesbian or gay friends, were not included.

Younger adolescents, those under 18 years of age, were also under-represented in the present study. Many of these adolescents are in the early stages of homosexual identity formation and do not yet possess a level of self-awareness that will propel them toward seeking the company and support of other lesbians and gays (Berger, 1983). However, research by the Kinsey Institute has shown that many gay men and some lesbians report homosexual feelings in their early adolescent years; typically, these feelings arise at age 13 for boys and at age 17 for girls (Bell, 1982).[1] These youngsters may benefit from contact with their peers in the lesbian and gay community and may want such contact. But younger adolescents face additional barriers: they may lack transportation, they may be less open with their parents about their homosexuality, more fearful that their parents will "find out" and more dependent on them for permission to attend a group or seek a service.

Under-utilization of lesbian and gay community services by younger adolescents should alert social workers, educators, helping professionals and family members to an unmet need. Lesbian and gay teenagers who must resolve homosexual identity formation concurrently with adolescent developmental tasks, may have little or no support and little accurate information about their development. In order to reach these youth, education of the general population about the full spectrum of sexual orientation is needed, as well as educational programs that will provide adolescents with nonjudgmental information about sexual identity and expression, interpersonal issues, sexual physiology and disease prevention.

Helping professionals must also be educated and prepared to recognize and assist with problems experienced by this group.

As in many surveys of homosexuals, lesbians were also underrepresented. One reason may be that lesbians tend to develop self-awareness about their sexuality at a later age than men (Moses & Hawkins, 1982, p. 47-48). But the authors' experience also suggests that lesbians prefer informal social networks to formal organizations and services, and they often perceive gay community organizations as male-dominated and insensitive to women's needs. Although most researchers agree that issues of psychosocial adjustment are different for lesbians and gay men, little is known about these differences. Certainly women have to deal with issues of sexism, both within and outside the gay community, as well as constricted opportunities for personal autonomy and career development. Men and women may also differ in their approach to intimate relationships and ways of seeking help. All this suggests that the social service needs of lesbian adolescents may differ significantly from those of their male counterparts. Differences based on sex were beyond the scope of this study, but certainly deserve the attention of future researchers.

Another area of concern is the family. Although most of the respondents in this study were 18 and older, the majority lived with parents or other relatives. Family problems were frequently cited, yet over half of respondents felt that parents were unhelpful or they were not sure if parents were helpful in resolving a personal problem. This suggests that the family is an arena where helping professionals could offer worthwhile interventions.

The most difficult family task is likely to revolve around the adolescent's disclosure of homosexuality and the family's initial and ongoing reaction to the disclosure. Lack of communication, misinformation about sexual identity, parental disappointments and long-standing family conflicts may combine to make this a particularly different family task (Silverstein, 1987). Even when parents accept the child's homosexuality, ongoing issues must be faced: should disclosure be made outside the family? How should the family react to the child's peer group or lover? How is the family to react to societal discrimination or disapproval?

The present research did not study those adolescents whose family conflicts were so severe that they decided to run away from home. But the literature suggests that a disproportionate number of runaways are lesbian or gay. We need more information about why adolescent lesbians and gays run, and what happens to them.

The data collected in this study did not support the observations of other researchers that lesbian and gay youth have a higher than average incidence of chemical dependency. Problems with alcohol or drugs were infrequent. In contrast, depression was reported by more than half of the respondents, although relatively few indicated that they had attempted suicide. Characteristics of respondents suggested a skewed sample, consisting of individuals successful in negotiating for formal and informal services within the lesbian and gay community. Problems with depression, suicide and chemical dependencies may be much greater among lesbian and gay youth without the friendship networks and organized group support which the individuals surveyed here enjoyed.

CONCLUSIONS

It is apparent that adolescent lesbians and gays continue to encounter negative experiences related to their sexual orientation, despite increased social awareness of homosexual lifestyles. Social service needs of these youths included assistance with identity management and control of disclosure of sexual orientation, depression, limited resources appropriate for dealing with their needs, and getting along with family.

Studies of the specific needs of adolescent lesbians and of younger adolescents of either sex are needed. In addition, continued assessment of the general needs of adolescent lesbians and gays, including drug and alcohol abuse, depression and suicide, and blocks to resource utilization will assist in recognition and prevention of problems encountered by this group.

Finally, implications for more effective professional intervention with this population included the need for continued education in the areas of lesbian and gay identity formation, homophobia, and appropriate referrals for adolescents who identify themselves as lesbian or gay. Social service providers and mental health practitioners must be aware of their lesbian and gay clients and be prepared to offer both supportive and practical services to them and their significant others. In this way, social workers and others may begin to counteract ignorance and negative social attitudes experienced by young lesbians and gays, and may assist in reducing their risk of encountering social and psychological problems.

NOTE

1. In a smaller study, Jay and Young (1979) found that 60% of gay men first realized their gay orientation from the ages of 9 to 15.

REFERENCES

Alyson, Sasha (Ed.). (1983). *Young, Gay, and Proud*. Boston, MA: Alyson Publications.

Baetz, Ruth. (1984). The coming out process: Violence against lesbians. In Trudy Darty and Sandee Potter (Eds.), *Women Identified Women*. Palo Alto, CA: Mayfield Publishing.

Bell, Alan P. (1982, November). Sexual preference: A postscript. *Siecus Report, XI* (2), pp. 1-3.

Bell, Alan P. and Weinberg, Martin S. (1978). *Homosexualities: A Study of Diversity Among Men and Women*. New York: Simon & Schuster.

Berger, Raymond M. (1982a). *Gay and Gray: The Older Homosexual Man*. Urbana, IL: University of Illinois Press. (Reprinted by Alyson Publications: Boston, MA 1984.)

Berger, Raymond M. (1982b). The unseen minority: Older gays and lesbians. *Social Work*, *27*(3), 236-242.

Berger, Raymond M. (1983). What is a homosexual? A definitional model. *Social Work*, *28*(2), 132-135.

Berger, Raymond M. (1987). Homosexuality: Gay men. In *Encyclopedia of Social Work* (18th ed.). Silver Spring, MD: National Association of Social Workers.

Bohn, Ted R. (1983/1984). Homophobic violence: Implications for social work practice. *Journal of Social Work & Human Sexuality*, *2*(3/3), 91-110.

CRUNCH Software. (1984). *Crunch Interactive Statistical Package Reference Manual*. San Francisco, CA: Author.

DeCrescenzo, Teresa D. (1983/1984). Homophobia: A study of the attitudes of mental health professionals toward homosexuality. *Journal of Social Work & Human Sexuality*, *2*(2/3), 178-183.

Fifeld, L. (1975). On my way to nowhere: Alienated, isolated, drunk. Los Angeles: Gay Community Services Center and Department of Health Services.

Garrison, Karl C. and Garrison, Karl C., Jr. (1975). *Psychology of Adolescence* (7th ed.). Englewood Cliffs, NJ: Prentice-Hall.

Gibson, P. (1982). Developing services to gay and lesbian youth in a runaway shelter. Gay Youth Counseling Manual. Unpublished manual, National Network of Runaway and Youth Services.

Gramick, Jeanine. (1983). Homophobia: A new challenge. *Social Work, 28*(2), 137-141.

Heron, Ann (Ed.). (1983). *One Teenager in Ten*. Boston, MA: Alyson Publications.

Hippler, Mike. (1986, September 16). The problems and promise of gay youth. *Advocate*, p. 42.

Jay, Karla and Young, Allen. (1979). *The Gay Report*. New York: Summit Books.

Lewis, Lou Ann. (1984). The coming out process for lesbians: Integrating a stable identity. *Social Work, 29*(5), 464-469.

Manaster, Guy H. (1977). *Adolescent Development and the Life Tasks*. Boston, MA: Allyn & Bacon.

Moses, Elfin A. and Hawkins, Robert O. (1982). *Counseling Lesbian Women and Gay Men: A Life Issues Approach*. St. Louis, MO: C. V. Mosby.

Orange County, Administrative Office. Program Planning Division. (1982). *1980 census report*. Santa Ana, CA: Forecast Analysis Center and Research and Planning Center.

Orange County, Board of Supervisors. (1985-1986). *Orange County progress report*. Orange County: Author.

Orange County, Health Planning Council. (1984). *Directions in behavioral health services*. Tustin, CA: Author.

Paul, William. (1982). Social issues and homosexual behavior. In William Paul, James D. Weinrich, John C. Gonsiorek & Mary E. Hotvedt (Eds.), *Homosexuality: Social, Psychological and Biological Issues*. Beverly Hills, CA: SAGE.

Price, James H. (1982, October). High school students attitudes toward homosexuality *Journal of School Health*, pp. 469-474.

Silverstein, Charles. (1977). *A Family Matter: A Parents' Guide to Homosexuality*. New York: McGraw-Hill.

United Way of Orange County. (1986, April). Orange County Needs Assessment. (Available from United Way of Orange County, P.O. Box 8130, Orange, CA 92664-8139.)

Vergara, Tacie L. (1983/1984). Meeting the needs of sexual minority youth: One program's response. *Journal of Social Work & Human Sexuality, 2*(2/3), 19-38.

Wasserman, S. (1976). Casework treatment of a homosexual acting-out adolescent in a treatment center. In Francis J. Turner (Ed.), *Differential Diagnosis and Treatment in Social Work* (2nd ed.). New York: Free Press.

Woodman, Natalie Jane and Lenna, Harry R. (1980). *Counseling with Gay Men and Women*. San Francisco, CA: Jossey-Bass.

Weinberg, George. (1972). *Society and the Healthy Homosexual*. New York: St. Martin's Press.

ADOLESCENT SEXUALITY IN RURAL AND URBAN AMERICA

Improving Family Planning Services to Rural Adolescents

Burton Mindick
Constance Hoenk Shapiro

SUMMARY. Individual differences among potential birth control users or among contraceptive clinic clients must be recognized in planning informative, persuasive, and effective birth planning programs. This article describes a longitudinal study conducted in three rural counties of upstate New York showing that contraceptive availability in the abstract is not enough.

The long-range goal of the research described here was to increase understanding of the psycho-social factors involved in adaptive human behavior as exemplified in the practice of fertility control. In order to do this, the authors measured both the characteristics of clinic users (or potential users) as well as those of the family planning clinics themselves in an effort to determine the extent to which individual differences and clinic characteristics contributed to the success of clients in following a plan of birth control.

Burton Mindick has been involved in birth planning-related research for some 16 years and has been an active member and officer of the Society for Population and Environment Psychology, Division of APA, by which he was recently honored for his contributions to the field.

Grateful acknowledgement is made to the Department of Health and Human Services Office of Population Affairs, and especially to Project Officer Dr. Patricia Thompson for support of this research to the authors under Family Planning Service Delivery Grant FPR 000035-02-0. Thanks are also extended to the research subjects and to the clinics and agency personnel for their patient cooperation. The authors are also grateful for the diligent efforts of research staff members Judy Burrill, Nina Cummings, Sandy Ehrlich, Ruth Kirlew, and Elie Molestad.

Availability of clinic services was considered to be potentially pivotal in the three rural counties where the research was conducted. With minimal public transportation, scheduling constraints imposed by school or family obligations, long distances to travel to the one clinic in each county, and often no telephone in the home, young women in the rural counties who desired family planning services faced barriers not usually experienced by their urban counterparts. It was hoped that the research findings might provide helpful data for rural clinics to use in an effort to maximize the effectiveness of their family planning services.

Previous research by other investigators in specific aspects of adaptive functioning and in the area of contraception as well as the first author's earlier studies in the same field, have led to the formulation of a theoretical model that conceptualizes developmental processes as they lead to the successful practice of birth planning (Mindick, 1978). But even more important, the model appears to be generalizable to successful human coping more broadly.

Briefly stated, the theoretical model (shown in Figure 1) implies that where early relationships, especially those between parent and child, lead to adequate internalization of societal norms and where

FIGURE 1

PROPOSED MODEL OF ADAPTIVE HUMAN FUNCTIONING

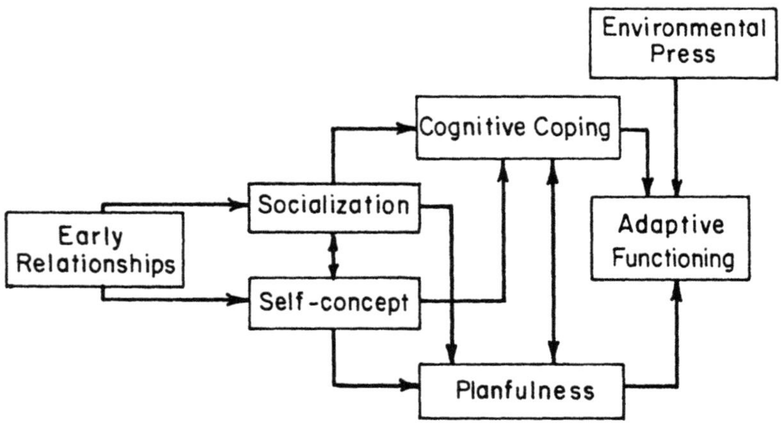

felt competence is an integral part of one's self-concept, the challenges of social living are met with an appropriate degree of information seeking (cognitive coping) and of planfulness. This results in attitudes and behaviors that are conducive to adaptive functioning in response to situational demands. At the simplest level of development, the model implies unidirectional causality. But as the model in Figure 1 implies, for later developmental stages, bidirectional causality and feedback loops are conceptualized, since, for example, successfully planful behavior may be expected to enhance self-esteem.

The basic elements of the theoretical model have received considerable empirical support in predicting birth planning in several studies of approximately 1100 urban clinic patients in southern California (Mindick et al., 1977; Mindick & Oskamp, 1982). Generalizability of the model to rural populations remained to be established. Testing of the model in the context of rural fertility patterns was especially important given recent findings of 15% higher fertility among young women in rural America than their urban or suburban counterparts (O'Connell & Rogers, 1982). Moreover, the model of adaptive coping is a complex one; and as successful as previous research may have been in obtaining significant relationships between its key concepts and success or failure in birth planning, a considerable proportion of the behavioral variance has remained unexplained.

In the last two decades, psychological researchers seeking greater theoretical explanatory power and better prediction have focused their attention on the interaction between persons and situations (e.g., Bem & Allen, 1974; Bem & Funder, 1978), especially in light of Cronbach's (1975) advocacy of interactionistic research generally, and Bowers' (1973) literature review which found that the person X situation interaction accounted for more behavioral variance than either main effect by itself. From the perspective of providing effective social services, this approach seems especially salient since the characteristics of services, of service recipients, and of the interaction between the two are particularly important (Chamie et al., 1982; Urban and Rural Systems Associates, 1976; Zabin & Clark, 1983).

METHODS

Research Design Overview

A three county-area in central New York State was studied to determine the differential impact of client characteristics or service characteristics or the interaction of these main effects that cause certain impoverished populations to be underserved in their contraceptive needs. The three counties were predominantly rural and contained large pockets of poverty. Unemployment rates were extremely high relative to nearby Tompkins County (where Cornell University is located), and the area is essentially an "Appalachia-North."

The study design targeted as research subjects four groups: (1) approximately 300 (100 in each county) randomly selected low income young women of child-bearing age who might or might not be using birth control; (2) service providers who regularly dealt with these women in the context of EFNEP, WIC, or pre-natal clinic programs; (3) a sample of 600 young women evenly distributed among the three counties comparable to group 1 but who were identified through their use of county family planning services during the first six months of premeasurement data collection; and (4) the service providers and clinics utilized by this second group of women as they initiated contraception or made return visits.

Our approach to the selection of contraceptive service users (or potential users) was determined by the need to study young women of childbearing age who alternatively might be *unserved, underserved, adequately served, or well served* with respect to their birth planning needs. This four-fold classification was then utilized to compare the self-reported personal, demographic, experiential and attitudinal characteristics of women in each of the service groups as well as their perceptions of the nature and extent of the services available to them.

Similarly, the two groups of service providers (those from the county family planning clinics as well as paraprofessionals rendering other direct services to the low income target populations) were asked to supply assessments of the characteristics of their clients as well as evaluations of the nature and extent of the family planning services available to these young women.

Thus, assessment of the main effects of personal characteristics or service characteristics or their interaction was carried out in multi-method fashion using eight major categories of data, which lent themselves to convergent validation. Service recipient characteristics, attitudes, and intentions were measured through two means: (1) responses to a brief interview conducted by a research team member and to short self-administered questionnaires, and other psychometric indices provided by the clients themselves; and (2) information provided by staff members who dealt regularly with these clients either in the EFNEP, WIC, or prenatal clinic, or in the three family planning clinics.

All the indices were intended to examine personality characteristics in accordance with the theory of adaptive coping put forward earlier, and tested in previous contraceptive research. All subjects were assessed in terms of their socialization, self-esteem, planfulness, and disposition to cope cognitively. Subjects also were asked about their experience, attitudes, and intentions related to fertility and contraception. In addition to these trait and attitude measures, subjects supplied information about themselves related to their demographic characteristics.

Beyond the psychometric and survey data collected from subjects who were users and non-users of family planning clinics, archival data were gathered from each family planning agency on all the clinic users who participated in this study. These data included the main elements of the contraceptive history of each clinic user from her initial visit over at least one year of birth control usage. Clinic records of the family planning service recipients were examined to study the relationship between their clinic usage patterns, their personal and demographic characteristics, and their expressed needs and attitudes toward birth planning services. The data collection focused on the following variables: (1) the kind of contraception chosen initially; (2) any changes in method; (3) the frequency and timeliness of return visits to the clinics; (4) any contraceptive side effects or other medical conditions reported to the clinic; (5) any pregnancies or births, and their wantedness or unwantedness; (6) change in marital status; and (7) clinic adherence, dropout, or transfer to another source for birth control. Criterion coding was then carried out to determine whether each clinic user had successfully met her own birth planning goals.

Measurement of Family Planning Characteristics

Parallel to the measurement of service recipient characteristics described just above was the assessment of the characteristics of the family planning services provided or available to low income young women in the rural areas being studied. Inquiry in this area was largely structured by a seven-part framework of evaluation questions put forth by Reynolds (1973). The seven basic areas of service delivery can be succinctly summed up in terms of the "what, who, when, where, how, how much, and why" of family planning efforts in the three counties being studied. Thus, interview and questionnaire measures were directed toward assessing: (1) the nature of the family planning services provided; (2) the kind of population served; (3) when these services are provided; (4) where in relation to the population served is contraception provided (including outreach efforts); (5) clinic processes by which contraception was provided; (6) the frequency of visits to the clinic and non-visit communications with the clinic; and (7) the likely reasons for the successes or failures of programs generally, or of elements within these programs.

Family planning services in each county were assessed through this framework both by clinic users and non-clinic users. Service providers, whether associated with the contraceptive clinic or other agencies, were also asked to describe and evaluate contraceptive clinic services. Finally, participant observation by a research team member was also employed to provide ethnographic data on processes of family planning service implementation.

Ethnographic Study of Process in Clinic Program Implementation

Observations in family planning clinics were carried out from the waiting room to the examining rooms, as staff members trained in participant observation methodology assisted in various aspects of the provision of services. Each of the research personnel spent approximately six months at one of the clinic sites, thus providing data on the commonalities and divergences in program implementation in the three rural clinics. The structure for these observations was the same seven-part framework used for quantitative evaluation of clinic sources.

RESULTS

Demographic Characteristics of the Total Sample

Age, Race, and Marital Status. The total sample obtained, both clinic and non-clinic, was the kind we had sought—young, both married and unmarried, and of low income status. Thirty-nine percent of the *total* sample were aged 13-17. Forty-five percent of the members of the *clinic* sample were of the same age group. Three-fourths of the total sample and four-fifths of the clinic sample were 25 years of age or younger, an age group that some experienced researchers on teenage pregnancy consider still in their adolescence. Virtually all such researchers consider this age group at greatest risk for unwanted pregnancy. Only about a tenth of the sample was in the 30 plus age group.

As expected in the areas of rural New York State studied, race was homogeneously Caucasian for all but three per cent of the total sample. Only one percent of the total sample was Hispanic, and in its non-white portion there was a comparably small number of Blacks and American Indians. Nearly half of the sample was single. Marrieds comprised about 30% of the subjects, and the marrieds together with those living with a sex partner formed a group of a size similar to the single group. Only a tenth of the total sample were divorced, separated, or widowed, a finding that is presumably associated with the young age of those studied.

Socioeconomic and Educational Variables. Modally, income ranged between $201-300 weekly. Most frequently this income supported three persons. Since about 70% of the sample earned approximately $15,000 or less annually and maintained at least three persons on this income, it appears that we were successful in our attempt to obtain a sample below or near the poverty level. Indeed, the respondent's own income was less than $15,500 annually in 95% of the cases, and nearly two-fifths of the sample had a family member currently on welfare at the time of the study's first wave of data collection. Nearly a fourth had had a family member on welfare in the previous two years.

Mothers and fathers from respondents' families of origin showed no distinct preferences in SES based on their job status, but three-fourths of the fathers and four-fifths of the mothers had completed no more than a high school education.

Multiple Regression Comparisons of the Clinic and Non-Clinic Samples

Our first set of inferential analyses compared subjects from the clinic and non-clinic samples in an attempt to determine the differences between women living in the same rural areas but who differ in their use of birth control services. To allow for control of appropriate variables and to help determine the relative contribution of the many variables and variable sets studied in accounting for clinic or non-clinic status, several multiple regression analyses were carried out. Using backwards elimination, multiple regression analysis was carried out upon the four basic variable sets, (1) demographics, (2) fertility-related attitudes and intentions, (3) clinic or county, and (4) personality characteristics.

The demographic variables showed the best predictive value with an R of .54, followed closely by the personality variables (R = .51), and the birth control attitude variables (R = .32). The regression on county had not even proven significant. Thus in combining the variable subsets, we began with what appeared to be the best predictors, the demographic variables and then added the personality variables.

When the two variable subsets were combined, the only demographic variables that remained significant were marital status (t = 2.19; p = .029), respondents yearly income (t = 2.29; p = .022), and the number of living children the respondent had (t = 4.48; p = .000). The clinic clients differed from the non-clinic subjects in being more likely to be unmarried, having a higher personal income, and having fewer children. As for personality characteristics, contraceptive clinic users had higher sex knowledge scores, but incorrectly estimated a conservatively larger number of fertile days in a woman's cycle. They expected to carry their education further and remained more optimistic about their future lives. Stein et al.'s (1968) Future Events Test (FET) discriminated between the two groups in showing that the non-clinic subjects gave more ages over all to FET events, expected more positive events "never" to happen (in line with their pessimism), and gave fewer ages for negative events. The total $R = .60$ for demographic and personality variables combined is a substantial one with $p = 0.000$.

Combining all of the relevant variable subsets, county, demographic, personality, and birth control, yielded an *R* of .64, again highly significant, but the analysis largely recapitulates the findings of previous analyses: geographical location (or clinic) was non-significant, clients had more affirmative birth control attitudes and stronger contraceptive intentions but were more apt to want to share contraceptive responsibility with their sex partners than the non-clinic subjects. The findings with regard to marital status, yearly income, and number of living children remained as in previous analyses, as does educational aspiration.

Once again the Future Events Test (FET) measures of optimism with the associated index of positive events "never" to happen as well as number of ages given for events generally and for negative events specifically continued as significant predictors in the directions previously described. One additional FET index emerged significantly in this final analysis of differences between clinic and non-clinic study participants – time horizon. This index which adds the mean future extension and the mean past extension measures of the FET (i.e., the average number of years for events backward and forward from the present age the respondent envisions) is a measure of the "time-bubble" in which the respondent lives. It is to some degree independent of age, which is perhaps why it emerged significantly in this last analysis when age and other suppressor variables were controlled. Theoretically, it should be the best measure of a person's ability to combine past and future into a "phenomenological present tense" (see Lewin, 1946) which allows an individual to use experience to plan wisely for future contingencies. In this final analysis the clinic group showed a significantly wider time horizon (t = −1.96; p = .05).

Multiple Regressions Comparing Successful and Unsuccessful Contraceptors

Multiple regressions similar to those for contraceptive clinic and non-clinic subjects were also carried out to determine differences between successful users of the contraceptive clinic and those who were unsuccessful in meeting their own contraceptive goals (i.e., had clearly unwanted pregnancies after having undertaken to use birth control). The results of these multiple regressions are complex and cannot be discussed at length due to space limitations. We may summarize the general findings, however, by pointing out that differences among the clinics providing contraceptive services appeared to explain the smallest amount of variance in contraceptive success or failure, achieving a combined R of only 0.056, p = 0.56, far from significant. Birth control attitudes produced an R of .30, p = 0.000. Next most important of the variable sets were the demographic which yielded an R of .36, p = 0.000. The personality variables provided the best prediction yielding an R of .59, p = 0.000. Indeed, the Future Events Test indices alone produced an R of .49, p = 0.000. Analyses of all of the variable sets produced a number of findings directionally opposite to our expectations, but generally speaking the hypothesized relationships posited by the theoretical model were by and large supported; and it was the personality variables, especially time perspective, that displayed the best prediction of success or failure in birth planning.

DISCUSSION

The above quantitative findings in discriminating both between users and non-users of contraceptive clinic services and between potentially successful and unsuccessful contraceptors lend further empirical support to the proposed theory of adaptive coping discussed earlier. More important, the success of the personological emphasis of the research and the small contribution of the situational variables have considerable theoretical and practical importance. For example, from the perspective of service provision, we were surprised that although there appeared to be marked differences in the effectiveness of clinic services as judged by our ethnographic observers, these differences did not seem to influence success or failure of the samples studied in terms of avoiding unwanted pregnancy. Both the quantitative and qualitative findings argue that given a certain minimum level of general service provision, *it is attention to individual differences among clients served that is likely to make a difference in client success or the lack of it*. This suggests that providing several specific services in rural family planning clinics might enhance their effectiveness in working successfully with adolescents. For young women who are assessed at intake as lacking sufficient motivation to carry through an effective plan of birth control, clinic personnel should plan intensive and individualized interventions, particularly in the area of education and emotional support aimed at increasing self-esteem. Following up on cancelled or failed appointments is also critical with adolescents who may still be quite ambivalent about their need for family planning services.

In situations involving unplanned pregnancies, young women who elect to terminate the pregnancy should be promptly helped to identify any problems that prevented them from maintaining their original plan of birth control. Adolescents who elect to carry an unplanned pregnancy to term should be encouraged to begin a new plan of birth control in the early postpartum period. In addition, since adolescents are generally less well informed about reproductive health issues than adults, it is particularly important for clinics to make a special effort to offer visits as opportunities to discuss with clients any dissatisfactions with their plan of birth control and to review and correct their knowledge of their own fertility and risks that exist to good reproductive health. It would be extremely worthwhile to encourage questions about the broader subjects of adjustment and life planning which are related to the model of adaptive human functioning which was the focus of this study.

Active outreach programs could potentially benefit adolescents who would not otherwise perceive a family planning clinic as sensitive to their unique needs. The important differences in attitudes toward birth control among clinic users and non-users as well as effective and ineffective users of contraception argue for stronger efforts to reach women of child-bearing age with programs designed both to inform and persuade about the considerable values of contraception and birth planning. The claim that contraceptive availability is sufficient to prevent unwanted pregnancy is not supported by the research. Attractive, individually nuanced, and outreaching programs appear to be necessary to close the service gap.

REFERENCES

Bem, D. J., & Allen, A. (1974). On predicting some of the people some of the time: The search for cross-situational consistencies in behavior. *Psychological Review*, *81*(6), 506-520.

Bem, D. J., & Funder, D. C. (1978). Predicting more of the people more of the time: Assessing the personality of situations. *Psychological Review*, *85*(6), 485-501.

Bowers, K. S. (1973). Situationism in psychology: An analysis and a critique. *Psychological Review*, *30*, 307-336.

Chamie, M., Eisman, S., Forrest, J.D., Orr, M. T., & Torres, A. (1982). Factors affecting adolescents' use of family planning clinics. *Family Planning Perspectives*, *14*, 126-137.

Cronbach, L.J. (1975). Beyond the two disciplines of scientific psychology. *American Psychologist*, *30*, 116-127.

Lewin, K. (1946). Behavior and development as a function of the total situation. In L. Carmichael (Ed.), *Manual of Child Psychology*, New York: Wiley.

Mindick, B. (1978). Personality and Social Psychological Correlates of Success or Failure in Contraception: A Longitudinal Predictive Study. Unpublished doctoral dissertation, Claremont Graduate School, Claremont, CA.

Mindick, B., & Oskamp, S. (1982). "Individual Differences Among Adolescent Contraceptors: Some Implications for Intervention." In I. R. Stewart and C. F. Wells (Eds.), *Pregnancy in Adolescence: Needs, Problems, and Management*. New York: Van Nostrand Reinhold.

Mindick, B., Oskamp, S., & Berger, D. E. (1977). Prediction of success or failure in birth planning: An approach to prevention of individual and family stress. *American Journal of Community Psychology*, *5*, 447-459.

O'Connell, M., & Rogers, C. C. (1982). Differential fertility in the United States: 1976-1980. *Family Planning Perspectives*, *14*(5), 281-286.

Reynolds, J. (1973). *A Framework for the Selection of Family Planning Program Evaluation Topics* (Manual for Evaluation of Family Planning and Population Programs, Manual No. 1). New York: Columbia University Division of Social and Administrative Sciences, International Institute for the Study of Human Reproduction.

Stein K. B., Sarbin, T. R., & Kulik, J. A. (1968). Future time perspective. *Journal of Consulting and Clinical Psychology*, *32*, 257-264.

Urban and Rural Systems Associates. (1976). *Improving Family Planning Services for Teenagers*. Washington, DC: U.S. Department of Health, Education, and Welfare, Office of Assistant Secretary for Planning & Evaluation/Health.

Zabin, L. S., & Clark, S. D. (1983). Institutional factors affecting teenagers' choice and reasons for delay in attending a family planning clinic. *Family Planning Perspectives*, *15*(1), 25-29.

Adolescent Fathers in Urban Communities: Exploring Their Needs and Role in Preventing Pregnancy

Edith M. Freeman

Societal ambivalence about sexuality in general has made it more difficult to clarify issues of adolescent sexuality, and to address those issues effectively. In the past, adult decisions about sexual involvement were often expected to result from mature judgement and commitment to a relationship. Even then, however, discrepancies were sometimes evident between a person's verbal agreement with the norm and what he or she actually did. The "sexual revolution" may have added to such conflicts inadvertently by reframing sexual involvement as an expression of freedom and individuality (Hite, 1987). The AIDS crisis and extremely high venereal disease rates have made this point of view less tenable today, yet adult patterns of sexuality that developed since the revolution have not changed substantially (U.S. Department of Health and Human Services, 1987).

Some adults experience stress from conflicts between old and new norms, while others have developed satisfying standards for themselves in spite of those conflicts. For many adolescents, with identity formation in transition, societal ambiguity has been problematic, particularly for *their* sexual identity issues. In fact, the Alan Guttmacher Institute (1976) notes that such ambiguity has led to higher rates of teenage pregnancy in the United States in comparison to other developed countries. Since the rates of sexual involvement for teens in this country and in other countries do not differ significantly, the high teen pregnancy rates in America are assumed to result from other contributing factors.

The Guttmacher studies conclude that one such factor in this country has been the fear that pregnancy prevention programs may encourage increased sexual involvement on the part of adolescents. As a result, some existing programs do not provide birth control services, while other programs have been eliminated in the planning stages. For teenagers who are already sexually active, this lack of resources has reduced their access to birth control measures and prevented what some authors characterize as sexually responsible behavior (Rosenweig, 1984).

Developers of innovative programs have, therefore, attempted to resolve conflicts about adolescent sexuality by teaching a range of sexually responsible behaviors. In these school- or community-based programs, the decision about whether to become sexually active is viewed as only one of many alternative ways to be responsible. Such programs usually provide comprehensive services to adolescent mothers and their infants, and to other young women who seem to be at-risk for early parenthood. Adolescent fathers and at-risk young men have not, however, often been included in these programs (Wallace, Weeks & Medina, 1982; Goldstein & Wallace, 1978). This has led to missed opportunities for providing additional resources to the mother-child dyad, and to young fathers themselves in terms of *their* needs (Rivara, Sweeney & Henderson, 1985). Moreover, such narrowly focused programs illustrate another societal bias about teenage sexuality: females are viewed as having major responsibility for the problem.

This article is focused on the above gap in services to adolescent males in urban communities. It reviews their developmental needs and the manner in which societal attitudes can affect their vulnerability to early parenthood and the resources in such communities. Finally, some examples of prevention programs for adolescent males are described to illustrate how social workers can enrich resource-limited communities and help provide less conflictual messages about adolescent sexuality.

YOUNG MALES WHO ARE AT-RISK

A narrow focus on pregnancy in isolation of the developmental context of the problem has not been effective in programs for young women (Freeman, 1987). This developmental context, along with society's struggle with adult *and* adolescent sexuality, must be considered in prevention programs for males. As conceptualized by various researchers, adolescent development includes the issues of friendship and loyalty, separation from the family of origin, career planning, courtship, and the formation of a functional identity (Freeman, 1987; Erikson, 1979). These issues are presented as adolescent males express them, with societal influences noted appropriately.

Hanging Out

Friendship and loyalty issues are typically referred to by young males as the ability to "hang out with peers." Decisions about values, priorities, and how to use leisure time are determined by peer consensus. Hanging out, however, means more than gaining peer acceptance: it also involves creating patterns of behavior that influence all important aspects of relationships with other young males. For instance, many studies indicate that adolescent males receive their first sex education from peers and spend most of their free time with those peers (Rivara et al., 1985; Hendricks, Howard & Caesar, 1981). Other authors note that most males, 11 to 13 years of age, believe peers influence their thoughts about sex and attitudes toward females as much or more than parents do (Freeman & Logan, 1987).

Moreover, Harford, Spiegler, and Freeman (1985) indicate that heavy drinkers among teenage males are usually introduced to alcohol by peers and drink primarily in the presence of peers at unsupervised parties. In comparison, abstainers or light to moderate drinkers may not be influenced as much by peers in this area. They are introduced to alcohol use by parents and more often drink at family gatherings or supervised parties. Finally, adolescents who drop-out of school tend to have more friends who are also drop-outs than young men who graduate from high school (Zarb, 1984). Both types of peer influence may indirectly affect sexuality. The use of alcohol at unsupervised parties may reduce inhibitions toward sexual involvement, and there may be added pressure on drop-outs to assume adult sexual roles.

Thus, hanging out with peers affords young males opportunities for decision-making that may not be available within their families of origin, at school, and in other life domains. Sexual expression is one area over which they have control and can use to influence the peer network. Those networks are also influenced by media messages about the macho image (what it means to be male) and its relationship to sexuality, although such messages are intended only for adult males. Any efforts to understand or change the emerging sexuality of these young men must, therefore, consider peer network dynamics and factors that influence the network.

Taking Charge of My Life

A second relevant area of development is separation from parents or as expressed by some young males "taking charge of my life." McRoy and Freeman (1986) define "separation as a normal and gradual process through which youth disengage and then depart from their families of origin." The process involves achievement of financial, functional, and emotional independence. When effective separation or differentiation of self from parents does not occur, adult status and the assumption of related responsibilities are delayed (Hewlett, 1984). When an appropriate level of separation from parents *is* achieved, individuals are able to maintain similar differentiated relationships with their family of procreation and with peers.

While this gradual process of separation is occurring, youth continue to be strongly influenced by the values and circumstances of family members (as well as those of peers). For example, Rivara et al. (1985) found that 77% of the mothers of teen fathers had been teenage parents themselves in comparison to 53% of non-father peers. In addition, 38% of the brothers and 45% of the sisters of teen fathers were adolescent parents (versus 24% and 43% respectively of the siblings of non-father peers). Significantly, Rivara et al. (1985) indicated that teen fathers in that study characterized their family's reaction to their parenthood as positive, while most non-father peers believed their family's reaction would be negative. Thus, in the circumstances of some teenage fathers, early parenthood may be a way of identifying with the family *and* initiating emotional separation at the same time.

This apparent strong influence of the family on young males' sexuality and potential for early parenthood must be considered in developing services for pregnancy prevention. Young males may not be sufficiently aware of this influence as they are attempting to take charge of their lives and separate from their families of origin. It may be necessary to help them to: (a) develop alternative ways of viewing their sexuality and potential parenthood, and (b) rechannel family support and identification toward more functional ways of separating.

Getting Ahead/Facing Life in General

Griffin (1987) noted "an area that is frequently and inextricately linked with separation by adolescents, particularly males, that of securing and maintaining employment." Only through financial independence can youth move toward the level of functional and emotional independence associated with maturity in young adulthood (Freeman & McRoy, 1986). Many young fathers and those at-risk for the problem have concerns about "facing life in general" and experience stresses from not being able to "get ahead" as expected in this society (Hendricks, 1983; Card & Wise, 1978).

High unemployment rates for both male and female youth within urban communities can prevent them from gaining early practical experiences in the world of work and information about related careers (McRoy & Freeman, 1986). Without such experiences, it is difficult to internalize the work ethic and a more mature attitude toward assigned responsibilities. Parents in depressed communities are also frequently affected by high unemployment rates for adults, making it less likely that they can provide credible advice about career planning. Further, they may be competing for many of the same jobs as the youth in their communities (Freeman & McRoy, 1986).

Currently, there is some controversy over who has major responsibility for career preparation: the school or the family. In some instances, this controversy has resulted in very little preparation, with each side assuming that the other is taking major responsibility for the task (Freeman & Pennekamp, 1988). Many young males who are at-risk for early parenthood live in out-of-home placements, which simply shifts this responsibility to some other large system. Included are foster care, juvenile detention, and residential treatment settings where problems in developing independent living skills among males have been well documented (Barth, 1986; Carpenter & Sugrue, 1984: Farrow & Schroeder, 1984: Griffin, 1987; Samulevich & Curcio, 1984).

In part, the male image has always been associated with financial independence. A community's failure to provide support and opportunities for developmental career planning, therefore, has direct consequences for young males. They are more likely to look for other avenues to assert their independence such as sexual expression, which can make them more high risk for early parenthood. If they become teenage fathers, they are less likely to provide financial and possibly emotional support to the mother and infant (Hendricks, 1983). In order to design effective prevention services, planners in urban communities must consider the relationship between sexuality issues among young men and the developmental task of "getting ahead."

Scoring or Getting Over

While authors refer to the fourth developmental task as courtship or relationships with the opposite sex, many teen males refer to it as "scoring." Another frequently used expression is "getting over" which is considered to be a way of asserting oneself in a society that does not otherwise seem to take young males seriously. This process of relating to the opposite sex has both sexual and nonsexual connotations. For instance, it can meet a young male's needs for intimacy and sexual expression. At the same time, it may also be linked to emotional aspects of a close relationship with a young woman or reinforce ideas of what it means to be a man. According to media messages and folklore, more assertive males are able to "get over" more often and are, consequently, considered to be more macho and effective.

Adolescent males are often less certain of their male image than adults because that image is in a developmental transition. As a result, they may be less knowledgeable about other types of male images or alternative ways to define their masculinity. Learning to make decisions about how to express their sexuality and the consequences of those decisions can also be difficult for young men (Moore & Hofferth, 1978; Rosenweig, 1984; Vadies & Hale, 1977). Prevention efforts can only be effective if they directly address male stereotypes and societal ambiguity about their sexuality, while providing meaningful opportunities for contact with adults who model alternative perspectives about masculinity. In this manner, "getting over" can be reframed by models significant to young men as the ability to convey a more caring image in opposite sex relationships.

Being Real

Underlying this need to "get over" and other developmental tasks is the central issue of identity formation. Young men typically refer to this as being yourself or "being real." Their goal is to express internal reactions honestly, allow others to see them as they really are, and to not get hooked by societal expectations that conflict with personal views. The desire to be real is a strength in many instances.

According to Freeman (1987), identity includes the self-concept, body image, racial identity, and sexual identity along with how one feels about those aspects of the self. Although many aspects of identity are formed during earlier stages of development, they are re-examined and modified during adolescence in light of that experience. The nature of identity modifications is influenced by other developmental tasks, such as peer relationships, and in turn identity influences these other tasks (Specht & Craig, 1982).

For instance, the lack of opportunity to obtain meaningful employment during and after school completion can impact negatively on the self-worth of adolescent males (McRoy & Freeman, 1986). This can produce stress from the struggle to be "up front" about how that makes them feel about themselves versus exhibiting a macho image which emphasizes that "nothing bothers me." Moreover, young males with identity problems that are manifested by a poor self-concept and psychological immaturity have been found to be particularly vulnerable to early parenthood and to exhibit problematic responses to this role transition (Elster & Panzanine, 1980).

In order to address the needs of young males through pregnancy prevention services, the interrelationships between these developmental tasks must be considered. This means that programs should help them to find other sources of self-esteem and to clarify the underlying connections between decisions about sexual involvement and their identity needs. The resources necessary for supporting positive identity formation are not always present in urban communities. Social workers can develop a process for analyzing resource availability as a beginning step in meeting the challenge within such communities.

THE CHALLENGE OF URBAN COMMUNITIES

Although social work has always emphasized the person-in-environment perspective, until recently, people's environments were viewed as rather passive contexts. Currently, both people and environments are viewed as having a dynamic growth and adaptive potential (Germain & Gitterman, 1980; Maluccio, 1979). The purpose of social work, based on this ecological perspective, is to engage the strengths and progressive forces within people and their environments when problems develop through discrepancies in the needs/resource balance (Meyer, 1984).

Within some urban communities, ranging from large metropolitan cities to suburban industrialized areas, there are many resource gaps for certain population groups, including young males (Mulvey, 1984). There is also great diversity: majority and minority youth, poor and middle-class families, and young and older adolescent males. This diversity presents opportunities to draw upon cultural and social class strengths in the development of adequate resources and coping patterns. Risks may result if similarities in the needs of young men, such as those from the previous section on development, are ignored and differences are used to compete for limited resources.

Assessment of the similarities and differences in needs is the first step which social workers can take in analyzing the adaptive capacities of young men within their communities. It can be done in written form or face-to-face encounters with representative groups of young men, family members, and other individuals in the community including informal leaders and professionals. Written questionnaires should be brief and simply written. It may be necessary to use a two-stage process in which needs are identified at a general level, the questions are refined and made more specific on the basis of that feedback, and the same individuals are asked to answer the more specific questions and to identify priorities. Whether using written or face-to-face methods, it is important to involve young men in deciding what to ask, and in gathering and analyzing the data.

Analysis should not only include what needs are identified and the priorities, but also differences and similarities in responses by various groups. Even when there seem to be differences, care should be taken to determine whether they are real. For example, there may be variations in how members of different racial groups or social classes express needs ("needing a place to hang out" may also be expressed as "needing time for myself"). The same needs may be perceived as requiring different solutions by different groups; adults may believe that young men can feel better about themselves by changing their personal appearance, while the young men may believe this can be achieved by having a job or being allowed to make more of their own decisions.

A second step in meeting the challenge of urban communities is analysis of the resources available for meeting the needs of adolescent males. The characteristics of resource-enriched and resource-limited urban communities are listed in the Appendix. Most communities have both types of characteristics and are more or less adequate in resources. The characteristics have been related to the developmental needs of adolescent males, but they may be equally relevant to the needs of young women and other population groups. In addition, similar characteristics can be used to analyze other types of communities even though urban communities contain certain idiosyncratic features.

For instance, the physical deterioration that occurs in some urban communities where large industries have moved out can affect the identities of youth in both the central and outlying areas of those communities. Germain and Gitterman (1984) have noted the negative impact from this lack of physical resources on self-image, dignity, and self-esteem. Urban renewal and changes in school district boundaries can isolate young men from their peer networks or positive adult role models. Such gaps in social resources can affect career planning, same and opposite sex relationships, and identity formation (Poole, 1984). Finally, if pregnancy prevention programs for adolescent males do not exist, are located in inaccessible areas, or do not involve creative outreach efforts, the target group may lack resources for learning about separation from parents or decision-making about sexual involvement (See Appendix) (Hendricks et al., 1981; Elster & Panzanine, 1980; Wallace et al., 1982).

To summarize, urban communities have characteristics that may enrich or limit the adaptive potential of young males. Resource availability is often affected by societal conflicts about their sexuality and competing national priorities. Analysis by social workers should focus on: (a) what resources exist in communities to meet the developmental needs identified by community residents (using the characteristics listed in the Appendix as guidelines), (b) what are the gaps in resources, (c) to what extent are resources being used appropriately, and (d) what strategies can be developed in consultation with young males to provide access to those resources or to create new ones?

MEETING THE NEW CHALLENGES: PRACTICE IMPLICATIONS FOR SOCIAL WORKERS

Implications for addressing the challenges of urban communities can be illustrated by a brief summary of two pregnancy prevention programs for adolescent males. In what was thought to be one rather homogeneous community, social workers from a private adoption agency and a school district decided to collaborate on concerns about a growing teen pregnancy problem. They planned a town meeting to which they invited teenagers from their self-esteem groups and a community recreation program, parents, and other individuals in the community.

The discussion from that meeting and follow-up interviews with some of the participants clarified similarities in needs as well as some differences. It also facilitated an analysis of community resources to meet those needs based on guidelines from the Appendix. As a consequence, two different pregnancy prevention programs were developed in the two areas of the community to address similar needs. Both programs were focused on teaching teens to be responsible about their sexuality, whether that meant abstinence, use of birth control measures, or other alternatives. One served a racially-diverse area, while the other served a primarily black area.

The latter area already had a viable prevention program for adolescent girls. Efforts to involve small numbers of males had failed in the past, so a program was designed to serve males. Social workers included the following components consistent with the needs and resources in the area: (a) facilitators included male sports figures, businessmen, and other community leaders suggested by the participants as positive role models, (b) the facilitators talked *with* the participants in their language about their areas of concern, while also encouraging a broad focus on many of their developmental needs in monthly sessions, (c) teens planned and taped radio/T.V. commercials and wrote articles in school newspapers about a variety of male role models, decision-making about sexuality, and destructive male stereotypes, (d) they were helped to examine how their racial identity and sources of self-esteem affected their views of what it means to be a male by using role plays and other exercises, (e) each youth was paired with a facilitator for help in finishing school/planning a career, gaining work experience, and beginning the process of taking charge of his/her life, and (f) natural peer networks were integrated into the same group sessions when possible.

In the second area of the community, a prevention program was designed for adolescent males and females, their parents, and service providers. While no comprehensive programs existed for pregnancy prevention, there was a loose coalition of agencies that provided services to adolescents including pregnancy counseling. Therefore, social workers developed a community forum format with sessions scheduled four times per year. The coalition and community members comprised the program's board, while funding was obtained from United Way and a small grant.

This program included the following: (a) forums involving a guest speaker, a film and discussion leader, or plays for living highlighting pregnancy prevention issues, (b) forums also included small group sessions in which male and female members talked directly to each other about the presentations and explored each others' ideas about the use of substances, leisure time, sexual involvement, finding a job, peer relationships, and family conflicts, (c) a teen advisory council of males and females helped to plan and monitor the program along with social workers in the coalition, wrote an advice column for other teens called "Growing Up and Facing Life," and served as peer counselors for small group sessions, (d) parents were periodically involved in small group sessions with other parents or teens around the transition of teens to adult roles and sexuality issues, (e) older siblings and parents of participants were often asked to discuss the consequences of teenage parenthood based on their own firsthand experiences, and (f) the coalition developed guidelines for follow-up with participants who needed more in-depth services and enhanced those services by observing the self-help strategies used by peer counselors.

CONCLUSION

Adolescent males have an important role in preventing teenage pregnancy. But they have often been excluded from services due to societal biases about teenage sexuality and the female's responsibility in this area. Social workers should become more knowledgeable about the developmental needs of adolescent males that have been discussed in this article. In addition, they should consider the impact of the urban environment on the males' development and the challenge this presents in providing effective services. Impacting societal biases through implementation of new social policies is equally important. Such multilevel interventions will undoubtedly require coalition-building between social workers, other concerned service providers and potential clients in urban communities, and policy-makers.

REFERENCES

Alan Guttmacher Institute (1976). 11 Million teenagers—What can be done about the epidemic of adolescent pregnancies in the United States? New York: Planned Parenthood Federation of America, Inc.

Barth, R. (1986). Emancipation services for adolescents in foster care. *Social Work*, *31*, 280-287.

Card, J. J. and Wise, L. L. (1978). Teenage mothers and teenage fathers: The impact of early childbearing on the parents' personal and professional lives. *Family Planning Perspectives*, *10*, 199-205.

Carpenter, P. and Sugrue, D. (1984). Psychoeducation in an outpatient setting: Designing a heterogenous format for a heterogenous population of juvenile delinquents. *Adolescence, 19.*

Elster, A. and Panzanine, R. (1980). Unwed teenage fathers: emotional and health educational needs. *Journal of Adolescent Health Care, 1,* 116-120.

Erikson, E. (1979). Life cycle. In Bloom, M. (Ed.), *Life span development.* New York: Macmillan, 19-29.

Farrow, J. and Schroeder, E. (1984). Sexuality education groups in juvenile detention. *Adolescence, 19.*

Freeman, E. M. (1987). Interaction of pregnancy, loss, and developmental issues in adolescents. *Social Casework, 68,* 38-46.

Freeman, E. M. and McRoy, R. G. (1986). Group counseling program for unemployed black teenagers. *Social Work with Groups, 9,* 73-90.

Freeman, E. M. and Pennekamp, M. (1988). Transitions from the world of school to the world of work. *Social work practice: Toward a child, family, school, community perspective.* Springfield, Ill.: Charles C Thomas Publisher.

Germain, C. B. and Gitterman, A. (1984). Education for practice: Teaching about the environment. Mimeo. New York: Columbia University School of Social Work.

Germain, C. B. and Gitterman, A. (1980). *The life model of social work practice.* New York: Columbia University Press.

Goldstein, H. and Wallace, H. M. (1978). Services for and needs of pregnant teenagers in large cities of the United States. *Public Health Reports, 93,* 46-51.

Griffin, W. (1987). *Independent living strategies: A program to prepare adolescents for their exit from foster or group care.* Tulsa: National Resource Center for Youth Services.

Harford, T., Spiegler, D., and Freeman, E. M. (1985). An ecological perspective on alcohol use among adolescents: Implications for prevention. In Freeman, E. M. (Ed.), *Social work practice with clients who have alcohol problems.* Springfield, Ill.: Charles C Thomas Publisher.

Hendricks, L. (1983). Suggestions for reaching unmarried black adolescent fathers. *Child Welfare, 53,* 141-146.

Hendricks, L. E., Howard, C. S., and Caesar, P. A. (1981). Help-seeking behavior among selected populations of black unmarried adolescent fathers. *American Journal of Public Health, 71,* 733-735.

Hewlett, G. (1984). Psychological separation of late adolescents from their parents. *Journal of Counseling Psychology, 25.*

Hite, S. (1987). *The new Hite report – Women and love: A cultural revolution in progress.* New York: Alfred A. Knopf.

Meyer, C. (1984). *Clinical social work in the eco-systems perspective.* New York: Columbia University Press.

McRoy, R. G. and Freeman, E. M. (1986). Family separation issues among black adolescents. Research report. Austin, Texas: University of Texas School of Social Work.

Moore, K. A. and Hofferth, S. L. (1978). *The consequences of age at first childbirth; Family size*. Washington, DC: The Urban Institute.

Maluccio, A. (1979). Promoting competence through life experiences. In Germain, C. B. (Ed.), *Social work practice: People and environments*. New York: Columbia University Press.

Mulvey, E. (1984). Delinquency cessation and adolescent development. *American Journal of Orthopsychiatry, 54*.

Poole, M. (1984). The schools adolescents would like. *Adolescence, 19*.

Rivara, F. P., Sweeney, P. J., and Henderson, B. F. (1985). A study of low socio-economic status, black teenage fathers and their non-father peers. *Pediatrics, 75*, 648-656.

Rosenweig, J. (1984). Adolescent sexual decision-making and guidelines for practice. Mimeo. Lawrence, Kansas: University of Kansas School of Social Welfare.

Samulevich, B. and Curcio, T. (1984). A vocational exploration program for residential youth. *Child Welfare, 54*.

Specht, R. and Craig, G. (1982). Adolescence: The search for identification. *Human development: A social work perspective*. Englewood Cliffs, New Jersey: Prentice-Hall, Inc.

U.S. Health and Human Services (1987). Acquired immune deficiency syndrome. Washington, D.C.: H. H. S. Department.

Vadies, E. and Hale, D. L. (1977). Attitudes of adolescent males toward abortion, contraception, and sexuality. *Social Work in Health Care, 3*, 169-174.

Wallace, H. M., Weeks, J., and Medina, A. (1982). Services for pregnant teenagers in the United States, 1970-1980. *Journal of American Medical Association, 248*, 2270-2282.

Zarb, J. (1984). A comparison of remedial failure and successful secondary school students across self-perception and past and present school performance variables. *Adolescence, 19*.

APPENDIX

Urban Communities:

Environmental Characteristics Related to the Needs of Young Males

Developmental Needs	Resource-Enriched Communities	Resource-Limited Communities
1. Same Sex Relation-ships - "Hanging Out."	Provide functional peer networks for decision-making, acceptance and influence (reciprocal) that facilitate development of mature judgments about use of substances, attitudes toward females and sexuality, school completion, and use of leisure time.	Provide peer networks that block the development of mature judgment (youth gangs, many out of home placements that limit decision-making, overly authoritarian school systems, etc.); or the structure isolates young males from more functional peer networks.

APPENDIX (continued)

2. Separation from the Family of Origin - "Taking Charge of My Life."	Supports exist for reinforcing early differentiation within families and adequate avenues for separation as a transition during adolescence: such as child care services, parent education (normative focus), life skills training throughout the developmental cycle, and functional male role models for natural helping efforts family-to-family.	Lack of resources for supporting early differentiation within families so that conformity to any dysfunctional family pattern is emphasized. Services provided may also support a focus on pathology. Patterns of family <u>and</u> community separation may emphasize traumatic leave taking and premature role transitions such as detention or early parenthood. Few role models of functional family relationships exist, and there is little energy for natural helping.
3. Career Planning -	Numerous opportunities exist for practical experiences in the world of work	Employment resources for adults and for adolescent males (in particular) are

"Getting Ahead/ Facing Life in General."	and career planning so that stress based on the role transition from school to work is minimal. Responsibility for this task is shared by several systems including the family, school, informal community leadership, and surrounding industries and professions throughout childhood and adolescence. In particular adequate male role models are available for facilitating the task.	minimal. Thus, competition is heightened between these groups and role modeling and mentorship for employment/career planning does not occur. There may also be competition for those resources between minority and majority group males or between various minority groups where differences are over emphasized (and there are barriers in the community to social contacts between groups). Available opportunities for employment and/or career planning may emphasize menial, low paying, and low status jobs with little hope for upward mobility while media messages equate high status, high paying jobs with a macho image.

APPENDIX (continued)

4. Courtship or Opposite Sex Relationships - "Scoring or Getting Over."	The peer network, family and community structures provide a range of sources of self-esteem and model equity in male/female relationships. Those resources counter media messages that equate assertiveness in opposite sex relationships with a macho male image. Educational and social policy resources (in the form of programs and services) provide a holistic perspective about opposite sex relationships beyond the aspect of sexual involvement.	The peer network, family patterns and circumstances, the media, and social policies reinforce premature role transitions into early parenthood and exploitation of females. Few community supports exist for alternative sources of self-esteem and intimacy other than sexual involvement.

5. Identity Formation - "Being Real."	Resources in the form of education and positive social contacts help adolescents to develop functional identities. Contacts may be with family members, adult and same-age role models and professionals with a non-pathological focus. Opportunities exist for young males to act on the environment successfully (problem-solve or prevent problems) in a way that makes them feel good about themselves (e.g., obtaining a job, doing something useful or pleasurable with leisure time, etc.).	Social contacts, education or the lack of education, and attempts to meet needs in the environment convey negative messages about the self-worth of young males. The physical environment may also reinforce a sense of hopelessness about the future and offer few sources of self-esteem. The lack of social and physical resources may support early parenthood as one way to express self or feel real.

Adolescent Sexuality and Premature Parenthood: Role of the Black Church in Prevention

Paula Allen-Meares

SUMMARY. This article calls attention to black adolescents and issues of sexuality and premature parenthood. Important developmental processes, including moral development and the fear of black genocide are discussed. Roles that the church can play in preventing premature sexual activity and parenthood are offered.

INTRODUCTION

My purpose in this article is to present some of the devastating consequences of adolescent sexual behaviors and premature parenthood with a particular focus on black adolescents. This discussion will also identify historical issues, unique to the black experience in the United States, which operate as barriers to preventive efforts such as the use of family planning services. Some of the developmental challenges common to adolescence are discussed, and the role that the black church can play in postponing sexual activity and parenthood is explored drawing upon relevant empirical studies. Social workers in both urban and rural areas should find this article useful, because it targets an institution that is rarely discussed but that has considerable potential in preventing premature parenthood.

I am not promoting any specific religious orientation or group (e.g., the New Right, or Right to Life) nor advocating abstinence as

This article was based on a paper presented at the Annual Conference of the AME Methodist Church, Champaign, IL, August 19, 1986.

the only acceptable sexual behavior; neither do I consider premature parenthood unique to blacks. What I am promoting is the notion that the black church is a very important institution in the lives of black parents and their offspring and as such should assume an educational role in this area. This position has evolved from an invitation to address 300 black missionary women wanting to know what the church could do to decrease the number of black adolescent pregnancies and early sexual experimentation. Perplexed by the problem, I explored the available literature, only to discover that not much had been written on this specific topic.

In the past, adolescents seeking information about sexuality have found greater support from their peers and have not viewed educational information received from formal or informal institutional structures as useful (Allen-Meares, 1984). Ideally, however, comprehensive programs to prevent adolescent pregnancy must involve many sections of the community (family, school, religious institutions), pooling their expertise to create an environment in which young people can learn responsible sexual behavior (Shapiro, 1980).

FACTS ABOUT SEXUALITY AND PREMATURE PARENTHOOD

In the United States today for all races combined, the mean age at menarche (the first menstrual period) is about 12.6 years. This is in contrast to 1940 when the mean age was 13.5 years (Planned Parenthood Federation of America 1986). More than 75% of girls begin to menstruate by age 13 and more than 96% by age 15. There is some evidence to suggest that minority girls begin menstruation and sexual activity earlier than whites (Chilman, 1983). Forty percent of young women become pregnant at least once before the age of 20 (Planned Parenthood Federation of America, 1986). Fewer than one in 50 teenage pregnancies is conceived within marriage. In 1981, 45% of teenage pregnancies were terminated by abortion, and in 1982, 46% of females 14 to 19 years of age had had sexual intercourse. Between 1971 and 1979 the percentage of females 15- to 19-years old having sexual experience rose by 25% overall and by 33% among the never married.

The percentage of young black women who have had intercourse has not increased since 1976 and has in fact declined since 1979, whereas the proportion of white adolescent women who have had intercourse increased up to 1979 and has hardly decreased since that time. Therefore, the gap in sexual experience between young white and black women has essentially diminished: the relative difference between the two groups was 300% in 1971; it is now only 23%. Those concerned with this particular problem contend that the underlying causes of teenage pregnancy are not racial, but social, and that the remedies needed are a society-wide responsibility, not merely that of one race, one group, or one institution (Planned Parenthood Federation of America, 1986).

Many younger adolescents wait an average of one year between initiating intercourse and first using a prescribed method of contraception. Older adolescents are more likely to use a contraceptive at first intercourse. They are also more likely to be using a highly effective method, mainly the pill. With some exceptions, the adolescent pregnancy rate in the U.S. is higher than that in many other developed countries for which data are available. The lower pregnancy rates in most other developed countries are attributable to higher levels of contraceptive use in these countries, rather than to a lower level of sexual activity (Planned Parenthood Federation of America, 1986).

The cost of adolescent childbearing and pregnancy can be devastating. It is costly for the child, the mother, the father, and for society in general. The young adolescent parent most likely will need support through public aid, other welfare programs, etc., and will require child care and other kinds of social services. A recent report estimated that the public cost in 1985 of adolescent childbearing was at least 16.65 million dollars (Planned Parenthood Association of Champaign County, 1986).

Further, the young adolescent parent is at risk. Both mother and father are likely to experience a difficult time completing school and will probably experience a life of economic difficulty. Also, infants born to adolescents have a greater risk of low birth weight and developmental delays, while the mother is at a greater health risk because of poor nutrition and inadequate health care (Furstenberg, Lincoln, & Menkin, 1981).

In response to this crisis, many states and different groups are drawing upon a variety of resources—from education, social service agencies, and community groups—to ascertain the extent of the adolescent pregnancy problem and determine the most effective ways to attack it (Planned Parenthood Federation of America, 1986). Many of us are very comfortable with clinics, schools, social service agencies, and the government having an active role in both prevention and intervention, but have often questioned the role of organized religion. What we must recognize is that the church and organized religion are powerful forces and resources in various communities and among certain racial and ethnic groups across the nation. In particular, the black church has always been the central institution within the black community. Historically, religious leaders have been and continue to be in the forefront of many social changes and movements (e.g., civil rights) (Nelsen, Yokley, & Nelsen, 1971). They have demonstrated their ability to motivate congregations and to bring about pressure to promote fair institutional and societal policies and practices. When I speak of mobilizing the church around this issue, I am advocating a cooperative venture involving social service agencies, relevant community groups, and the religious community.

DEVELOPMENTAL PROCESSES

The physical changes that begin at puberty signal the start of a host of psychological and psychosocial challenges. Identity is one of these challenges. When asked how important it is to "feel good about myself," three of four adolescents gave this top priority. Aside from this common identity of feeling good about oneself, however, gender difference takes on more significance. It is still believed by some that girls have a much more difficult time accepting their various physical and psychological changes (Planned Parenthood Federation of America, 1986). The satisfaction of boys with their bodies tends to remain stable from grades 5 through 9, whereas girls' satisfaction declines during this period.

Another major developmental challenge for young adolescents is intimacy. Meaningful relationships with others require social skills and the ability to self-disclose. Further, the ability to empathize and to make friends are other skills that take on importance in relationship building. In one study, ninth-grade girls could apparently connect with others intuitively better than boys could. Also, the premarital chastity standard was valued more by girls than by boys. One in five ninth graders reported that they had experienced sexual intercourse, with twice as many boys as girls being nonvirginal. It is difficult to determine whether this behavior reflects their personal values and experiences or those of their parents. It is also possible that boys feel more pressure to report sexual activity, even when they may not have had it. That means that data collected on this topic must be viewed with some skepticism.

Related to the development of personal values is moral development, reasoning, and self-regulation. This is a very complex topic and beyond the scope of this discussion. However important the aspect of moral development may be, it is frequently ignored in discussions about adolescent sexuality. A review of Sebes and Ford (1984) offers several insightful conclusions abstracted from three decades of empirical studies on moral development, with Kohleberg's (1969) work as a cornerstone. Their conclusions are that (a) there are multiple forms and content of moral reasoning used by every group studied; (b) normative forms used by groups vary from age to age and within every culture and age group studied; (c) individuals vary in form and content of moral reasoning used at every age; and (d) moral reasoning seems heavily influenced by situational variability. Thus, moral development can be understood only within its behavioral and situational context.

When applying these conclusions to adolescent sexuality and premature parenthood among blacks, it is important to note the possible variance in moral development specific to culture and age and the situational contexts in which development takes place: in other words the black experience in America. To develop interventive and preventive programs, one must recognize and incorporate these factors into such efforts.

Kavolis (1977) states:

> While various kinds of collective moral structures can be identified in the historical record, the most encompassing structure

> of moral experience can be conceived of as a "moral culture." Moral cultures are constellations of emotions and ideas, occurring within identifiable collectives, pertaining to the basic responsibilities and limitations of human beings. . . . Any moral culture also contains, explicitly or implicitly, a particular "package" of moral logics, which are guidelines for acting with regard to right-wrong distinction. (p. 331)

In most books on child and adolescent development and psychology, little attention is paid to the role of religion. Nevertheless, one survey found that the vast majority of American children and their parents are involved in some way with religion. A recent Gallup poll shows that 74% of youth 13 to 15 years of age say that religion is the most important, or one or the most important influences in their lives. Ninety-five percent believe in some universal spirit, 60% of American parents of children under the age of 18 say that their children are currently receiving some form of religious instruction, and 83% of American adults maintain that they would want a child of theirs to receive religious instruction (Forliti & Benson, 1986).

BLACK GENOCIDE

Contrary to popular belief, empirical studies do document that many blacks endorse family planning services (Elifson & Irwin, 1972). Over the years some blacks have expressed suspicion of the dominant society's advocacy of birth control, judging it to be a tactic of genocide. This is not believed to be a current barrier for confronting premature parenthood among adolescents.

Genocide and population size are issues of relevance to any minority group, particularly when the dominant society is perceived as hostile. During periods of turbulent race relations, this concern has surfaced. For example, in 1973, Turner and Darity wrote of an increasing concern in the black community that birth control (family planning) programs were perhaps a method of black genocide. They placed this fear within the context of black America's historical roots; specifically, the centuries of brutalization (lynching, castration, etc.) at the hands of the dominant group. Also, while compulsory sterilization proposals, appearing primarily in southern states at the time, had the explicit intent of reducing the welfare rolls, some believed that the implicit motivation was elimination of a race. Thus, the argument continued, the perceived intent was to encourage blacks to use birth control to eliminate and minimize the presence of this group in society. Perplexed and concerned about this thinking, Turner and Darity conducted a study to investigate the extent of genocide fears among a large regionally varied group of black Americans. The findings of their study indicated that genocide fears were widely held in the black population and that factors of age, sex, region and educational level were related to the prevalence of this fear. On all items the younger respondents expressed more fear than the older group. Males expressed more fear than females, and all respondents with less education expressed greater fear. Of the sample, 39% believed that birth control programs were a genocidal technique. Though respondents were not against family planning programs, they were suspicious of the intent by the dominant society. The ambivalence created by fear of genocide and the desire to use contraceptives is clear. From these findings one could conclude that fear of genocide could be one barrier to the effective use of contraceptives among young black Americans.

Perhaps more attention to and concern about black adolescent sexuality should come from within the black community. This issue must be placed within the context of contemporary reality, that is, concern for adequate nurturing and socializing of babies born to adolescents and the consequences of premature parenthood for the young parents. One of the logical institutions to address these issues within the black community is the church.

RECOMMENDED ROLES FOR THE BLACK CHURCH

Why should social workers and others concerned with this issue consider nurturing and developing the role of the black church as a preventive resource? More than half of the black community in America has some identifiable church connection, and 90% of that population claims allegiance to a church (Jones & Matthews, 1977; Walters & Brown, 1971). Further, the church and its congregation must remember that the contemporary black church does not exist in a vacuum; it exists in a social context. Therefore, it too must be sensitive, take a leadership role, and be cognizant of social problems. The church, which cuts across various denominations, has been the focal point not only of spiritual fulfillment, but has also offered an arena for community participation, social activities, and socialization of its members, and has provided comfort and assistance in times of crises. The church reveals a tremendous potential for alleviating a number of social problems. The influential role of the black minister has long been recognized. Typically, ministers serve in different capacities, fulfilling the roles of educator, counselor, and program developer, among others (Berenson, Elifson, & Toller, 1976).

I propose that the black church should assume a leadership role by developing educational programs that address sexual development from childhood through adolescence. Surely, there will be some opposition to the following suggestions, but the promotion of an educational stance as a strategy to prevent premature sexual activity and parenthood is documented by empirical evidence and would probably be welcomed by most parents. It has been shown that black adolescents who have had some exposure to sex education are more likely to use some method of contraception once they become sexually active (Zelnik & Kim, 1982).

The specific thrust and focus of an educational intervention strategy that the black church can draw upon can be found in the literature. The literature suggests that effective parent-child communication (particularly between mother and daughter) around sexual issues is critical to postponing sexual activity among adolescents (Fox, 1981). The black church could organize workshops for parents and/or the adolescent's significant others on how to communicate effectively the facts about sexual development and the consequences of sexual activity. Such an effort should depart from tradition and involve both parents, whenever both are available. It is also important to involve adolescents and parents/significant others in the same group in order that mutual communication skills be learned and practiced by both.

As a part of the church's youth program, workshops can be organized for preadolescents and adolescents that address the realities of sexual, physical, emotional, and moral development, and the consequences of sexual intercourse. Further, these workshops should include an opportunity to learn a variety of social skills. Drawing upon the groupwork approach, youth should be taught responsible decision-making and interpersonal skills by using realistic role playing and situations that they will encounter in life. Adolescents must have the facts to make responsible decisions, but they also need an opportunity to apply what they have learned to specific situations (Schinke, Gilchrist, & Small, 1979). This effort must include both males and females; too many programs have ignored the male's role (Shapiro, 1980).

In addition, it has been found that those adolescents with educational aspirations are more likely to postpone parenthood (Chilman, 1983). Given this fact, the black church's programming should include career and educational guidance that targets its youth and their parents. If the church lacks the expertise to organize this effort, it should draw upon community resources. Guidance counselors and social workers from the local schools and community persons representing a variety of careers and professions could be invited to assist with this effort.

I believe that the black church can be of key importance in the network of agencies and institutions to prevent adolescent pregnancies. To discount or exclude this institution as an ally in this effort is to waste a valuable resource.

REFERENCES

Allen-Meares, P. (1984). Sexually active adolescents: Implications for social work intervention and family planning. *Journal of Social Work & Human Sexuality*, *3*, 17-26.

Berenson, W., Elifson, K., & Tollerson, T. (1976). Preachers, in politics: A study of political activism among the black ministry. *Journal of Black Studies*, *6*, 373-391.

Chilman, C. (1983). *Adolescent sexuality in a changing American society*, New York: Wiley.

Elifson, K., & Irwin, J. (1977). Black ministers' attitudes toward population size and birth control. *Sociological Analysis: A Journal of the Sociology of Religion*, *38*, 252-257.

Forliti, J., & Benson, P. (1986). Young adolescents: A national study. *Religious Education*, *81*, 199-224.

Fox, G. (1981). The Family's role in adolescent sexual behaviour. In T. Ooms

(Ed.), *Teenage Pregnancy in a family context: Implications for policy*. Philadelphia: Temple University Press.

Furstenberg, F., Lincoln, R., & Menkin, J. (Eds.) (1981). *Teenage sexuality, pregnancy, and childbearing*. Philadelphia: University of Pennsylvania Press.

Jones, D., & Matthews, W. (Eds.) (1977). *The black church: A community resource*. Washington, DC: Institute for Urban Affairs and Research, Howard University.

Kavolis, V. (1977). Moral cultures and moral logics. *Sociological Analysis*, *38*, 331-344.

Kohleberg, L. (1969). Stage and sequence: The cognitive development approach to socialization. In D.A. Goslin, *Handbook of socialization theory and research*. Chicago: Rand McNally.

Nelsen, H., Yokley, R., & Nelsen, A. (Eds.) (1971). *The black church*. New York: Basic Books.

Planned Parenthood Association of Champaign County. (1986). *Issues*. Champaign, IL.

Planned Parenthood Federation of America. (1986). Teenage pregnancy: The search for solutions. *Planned parenthood review*, *6*, 1-41.

Schinke, S., Gilchrist, L., & Small, R. (1979). Preventing unwanted adolescent pregnancy: A cognitive behavioral approach. *American Journal of Orthopsychiatry*, *49*, 81-88.

Sebes, J., & Ford, D. (1984). Moral development and self-regulation: Research and intervention planning. *Personnel and Guidance Journal*, *7*, 379-382.

Shapiro, C. (1980). Sexual learning: The short-changed adolescent male. *Social Work*, *25*, 489-493.

Turner, C., & Darity, W. (1973). Fears of genocide among black Americans as related to age, sex, and region. *American Journal of Public Health*, *63*, 1029-1034.

Walters, R., & Brown, D. (1971). *Exploring the role of the black church in the community*. Washington, DC: Mental Health Research and Development Center Institute for Urban Affairs and Research, Howard University.

Zelnik, M., & Kim, Y. (1982). Sex education and its association with teenage sexual activity, pregnancy and contraceptive use. *Family Planning Perspectives*, *14*, 19-25.

Networking with Rural Adolescents and Their Parents to Promote Communication About Sexual Issues

Constance Hoenk Shapiro

SUMMARY. The strengths and limitations of rural communities must be carefully assessed when planning programs that depend upon local participation. This article describes a sexual learning program that utilizes natural helping networks to build support groups of pre-teens, adolescents, and their parents.

In spite of rising rates of adolescent pregnancy and sexually transmitted diseases in rural communities, efforts to implement preventive programs have not been as well funded or as widespread as those in urban areas. In part this may be attributed to the caution that rural communities display when articulating their needs; sexual issues are often presumed to be the responsibility of the family or the church rather than government or private funding sources. Then, too, many rural communities have other pressing needs that demand attention, enabling them to deny the compelling nature of the problems young people face in the area of sexual learning. Social workers familiar with developing intervention programs in rural areas are aware of the importance of starting where the client is, utilizing local community leaders, developing existing resource systems, emphasizing family involvement, and encouraging skills in self-sufficiency valued by many rural residents. This article describes a rural family sex education program that utilizes local leadership and community networking strategies to build support groups of pre-teens, adolescents, and their parents.

NATURAL HELPING NETWORKS

The existence of natural helpers has long been recognized as a crucial resource in rural communities (Collins & Pancoast, 1976; Bedics & Doelker, 1983; Davenport & Davenport, 1982). In communities grappling with such limitations as poor transportation, social isolation, a dearth of social agencies, and a suspicion of outside service providers, it is important also to acknowledge the existing strengths: concern for one's neighbors, ability to mobilize human resources, awareness of interlocking social networks, and the desire to work toward stability in family life. Importance is placed on the family, and institutions such as the school, church, and local organizations usually provide the locus of community activity. Face-to-face and community activities are preferred (Skaggs, 1971), thereby validating the importance of utilizing social networks when developing and implementing programs. Social workers have utilized natural helpers in rural communities to develop preventive programs on child abuse (Andrews & Linden, 1984), battered women (Yoder, 1980), acquired immune deficiency syndrome (Rounds, 1988; D'Augelli & Hart, 1987), and rural health care issues (Dotson, 1981). In addition, sex educators traditionally have relied on natural helpers in school settings, on youth hotlines, in family planning clinics, and in youth organizations (Shapiro, 1981).

One of the advantages social workers find in working with natural helpers is that those individuals are already familiar with local resources. In addition, natural helpers are also aware of such crucial issues as how to involve local participants, what issues will mobilize local citizens to action, and what level of involvement it is reasonable to expect of concerned citizens. Rural residents are accustomed to involving others in projects of importance, and they have a good sense of how to work cooperatively so that many people's needs can be met simultaneously. By understanding the power of natural helpers in rural communities, social workers can tap into an already existing network of action-oriented citizens and, working hand-in-hand, develop programs that are well-suited to the perceived needs of community residents.

SEXUAL LEARNING

Sex education in the United States has been fraught with difficulties over the years. Initially sex educators needed to confront the public's assumption that sex education would make young people promiscuous and would encourage them to experiment with sexual behaviors that would otherwise not have occurred to them. Schools often were reluctant to incorporate curricula on sex education, fearing both parental opposition and reluctance of teachers who felt unprepared to deliver content in the sensitive area of human sexuality. The usual result has been to address human sexuality as a unit in a health or a biology course, with more of an emphasis on physiology than on the equally compelling socio-emotional issues.

Studies of sex education have looked at course effectiveness, methods of teaching, and the qualifications and attitudes of potential instructors. By far the greatest number of studies are reports of attempts to measure the impact of sex education courses on knowledge, attitudes, and behavior of students (Kirby, Alter & Scales, 1979). These studies tend to point out the inconsistency of curriculum goals and evaluation techniques, thereby making more difficult the task of assessing the impact of sex education efforts. What is clear, however, is that sex educators tend to target their efforts at groups of young people, often neglecting the opportunity to make contact with parents as well. Yet parents, much as they may articulate the wish to be the primary sex educators of their children, are equally ready to acknowledge feelings of discomfort when faced with such a task. Study after study reveals that parents, especially fathers, feel awkward talking with their children about sexual issues and, as a result, provide very little information that young people find helpful (Shapiro, 1981, p. 54).

In the 1980s, concern with the rising rates of unplanned pregnancies has caused some agencies to develop innovative approaches, usually generated from dissatisfaction about existing learning opportunities available in the community. These efforts, often isolated, dependent upon short-term grant funds, and closely identified with the sponsoring agency, have the potential to be creative, but have the disadvantage of minimal carry-over to the community once funding disappears. An additional problem with many programs is the emphasis on pregnancy prevention, as opposed to conceptualizing the challenge more broadly as one of sexual learning.

An emphasis on sexual learning has the advantage of including participants of various ages and family groupings, as well as being able to address issues from a bio-psycho-social perspective. Sexual learning is broader than sex education, in that it includes the acquisition of attitudes, values, and behaviors, as well as information (Shapiro, 1981). In addition, because sexual learning tends to be an unfolding process, as opposed to rigid adherence to a prescribed curriculum, participants can bring their own questions and concerns to the group, where there is an expectation that the interactive process will enrich the curriculum. Furthermore, as participants increasingly are invited to make their needs known and to find ways of meeting those needs, the process of sexual learning can become an empowering experience for young people and parents alike. In rural communities, a family approach to sexual learning is compatible with many already existing values that stress family involvement, encourage parental leadership, and emphasize self-sufficiency among all family members.

THE FAMILY LIFE DEMONSTRATION PROJECT

The Family Life Demonstration Project was developed with a unique appreciation for the values of rural communities. Funded by the Office of Adolescent Pregnancy Programs (U.S. Department of Health and Human Services) and sponsored by the Rochester Diocese of the Catholic Church, the project was implemented in two rural communities in the northeastern United States. The project was begun in the belief that prevention is the best way to demonstrate concern for the rising rates of adolescent pregnancy and sexually transmitted diseases that were identified in the targeted rural communities. Its emphasis on using natural helpers to work with family units over an 18 month period enabled this project to be particularly well suited to the needs of rural communities.

Designed with the goal of empowering community participants through access to local resources, the project emphasized mastery of new skills according to a model originated by Mindick (Mindick & Oskamp, 1982). It stressed affirmation of the family unit and was attentive to the ongoing needs of participants, constantly involving them in planning, revisions, and program delivery efforts. The accent on refining communication skills, identifying community resources, and mobilizing latent leadership within the group enabled participants to assume an increasing amount of responsibility for their progress over the duration of the project. The approach was markedly influenced by Mindick's (1986) work on effective and ineffective strategies of program implementation.

Recruitment

The use of natural helpers was crucial to the evolution of the group members as active participants in the learning process. Once the demonstration grant was funded, efforts were made to identify local members of the community who were considered natural helpers; in other words, those people to whom others turned in times of trouble and who gave willingly of themselves to their friends and neighbors. Once hired, the two group leaders were given the responsibility for publicizing the Family Life Demonstration Project throughout their communities. Whereas traditional methods of publicity would have involved newspaper advertisements and radio announcements, the group leaders went to the heart of their rural communities by placing brochures in laundromats, local gathering places, family health clinics, and community bulletin boards. In addition, since face-to-face communication was recognized as important, especially given the sensitivity of the content on sexual learning, the group leaders made announcements to religious congregations, visited grange meetings, spoke at PTA meetings, held community meetings to elicit input from interested citizens, and encouraged their friends to "spread the word." Interestingly, the husbands of both group leaders became involved informally from the very beginning, as each spoke with pride around the community of his wife's new job and the importance of her responsibilities.

Scheduling

Once the recruitment efforts had concluded, 50 families in each of the two sites had committed themselves to an 18 month involvement with the program. Families with preteen and adolescent children were eligible, and meetings were scheduled to maximize the participation of fathers as well as mothers. Three all day Saturday workshops were scheduled at 6 month intervals and, at the request of the families, workshops were not scheduled during planting or harvesting seasons, nor during summer vacations. To supplement the learning that occurred at the all day workshops, 2 hour "enrichment" meetings were scheduled at monthly intervals in the evenings at the families' convenience. Since many of the rural families began their days early, the evening sessions were scheduled so that families could be home by 9:00 p.m. The 50 families in each site were divided into groups that included between 5 and 10 families apiece. These families then remained together for the duration of the project, setting group learning goals and initiating experiences that would contribute to the overall learning of the group.

Content

Each of the three all day workshops was organized around learning objectives articulated by participants in their early contacts with the group leaders. The curriculum of the workshops was designed by the author to provide opportunities for parents and young people to talk about attitudes and to find satisfying ways of interacting, particularly around conflictual issues (Shapiro, 1987). In addition to teaching specific communication skills, such as asking open-ended questions, paraphrasing statements, stating needs assertively, asking for and giving feedback, and negotiating, the workshops also emphasized process skills, such as values clarification, decision making, conflict resolution, and locating resources necessary to ongoing sexual learning. In addition, content on anatomy, reproduction, contraception, sexually transmitted diseases, and physical development was covered, both through small group exercises and with the help of handouts given to each family to keep for easy reference.

The monthly enrichment meetings were perceived by participants as a time to go beyond the content covered in the all day workshops and develop learning goals that reflect the unmet needs of the group. Although the group leader was present for each monthly enrichment meeting, her role was to encourage participation and leadership from group members. With the group leader assuming the role of a facilitator, members were encouraged to take responsibility for meetings by identifying topics of interest, inviting guest speakers, bringing in resource materials, leading group discussions, or participating in other ways to help the group reach its learning goals.

Young people were especially encouraged to participate, as a way of offering an alternative to the group's original assumption that the adults would take major responsibility for shaping the direction of the group. Occasionally this resulted in the group dividing by generations into separate discussion groups, but more often parents and their children identified shared areas of interest and were able to divide the responsibility for carrying out the evening's program.

Most topics identified by the group were directly related to sexuality, although others were related more broadly to issues involving self-esteem and identity. Young people and their parents used enrichment meetings to learn about and to discuss such issues as substance abuse, suicide, and eating disorders, in addition to the more familiar topics related to sexuality.

Process

In terms of process, the workshops offered a variety of ways of presenting material and stimulating discussion of content. Lectures were rare, and when they occurred, they were brief and interspersed with visual illustrations, handouts, and personal examples to emphasize the point being made. Small group exercises were a favorite among participants, as were films and other audiovisual materials. Role playing was initially perceived as awkward, but the participants demonstrated greater comfort with this technique when it was first modeled by the group leader.

A regular component of every group meeting was opening the question box, a repository for questions that people preferred to submit anonymously. There would be a specific time set aside during each session when the leader would read the questions to the group, encouraging others to volunteer answers. If the question could not be answered by someone in the group, a member would be asked to volunteer to find the answer in time for the next monthly enrichment meeting. Suggestions regarding where the volunteer might search for information were encouraged in the group, thereby enabling everyone to share responsibility for being active participants in the learning process. In the first six monthly meetings, there were always questions in the box, but following the second all day workshop it was unusual to find people using the question box, in large part because of their increased comfort in asking questions, and in part because many answers to their questions had already come up in the course of the group discussions.

Research on transfer of learning has shown that practice of a newly learned behavior will increase its application in situations away from the original learning environment (Rose, 1973). With the awareness that many of the rural participants were learning skills that were unfamiliar, the group leader sought to increase the level of familiarity by providing "booster activities." The group leaders were supportive of giving participants small assignments to be carried out at home, but they were united in discouraging such assignments from being called "homework," so the term "boosters" was coined instead. This euphemism for monthly homework referred to fun family exercises that depended upon the use of a newly learned skill. Families were encouraged to report back at the next meeting how their experiences with the booster exercises had gone, and the general response to these practice sessions was positive. Inevitably, the group leader would ask participants to volunteer examples of ways they had used new behaviors in their everyday life, thereby emphasizing that the "boosters" were to be viewed as an approximation of behaviors that would ultimately feel increasingly comfortable with practice.

In an effort to avoid having the adults monopolize discussion in the workshops and monthly meetings, teen facilitators from the groups were identified by the group leaders and invited to assume some leadership responsibilities in the group meetings. Selected because of their good interpersonal skills and their interest in learning about sexuality, the teen facilitators were very helpful in encouraging discussion by their peers and in modeling appropriate involvement by young people in the work of the group.

Volunteer Training Sessions

Every 3 months, training sessions were made available to any group member who indicated an interest in helping to facilitate evening enrichment meetings or exercises during an all day workshop. Although any group member could offer to take responsibility for some aspect of a group, many participants indicated that some rehearsal in advance would enable them to feel more comfortable about volunteering their efforts. Young people and parents utilized the training sessions to learn leadership skills, to refine specific presentations in a supportive group, and to explore new ways that their participation in the group could maximize its learning goals.

Group Leader Training

Since the two group leaders were pivotal people in their groups, particular attention was given to their needs. Initially unfamiliar with the curriculum content of the all day workshops, the leaders articulated their need to know more about both content and process. They met regularly with the author, both to specify the learning goals of their groups, and also to learn specific instructional strategies that they might utilize (Shapiro, 1987). As these meetings evolved, the author found them as valuable as did the group leaders. With instant feedback about the usefulness and relevance of the curriculum, it became possible to make a variety of practical revisions that contributed to the ultimate success of the final curriculum.

Outcomes

At the point in the project when all groups had completed two all day workshops and between 12 and 18 enrichment meetings, the funding of the Family Life Demonstration Project was abruptly terminated. The sponsorship of the project was perceived as violating constitutional mandates for separation between church and state and, without funds, the project staff informed families that it would be unable to continue its work with them. Although the project had an evaluation component in place, the abrupt ending precluded the possibility of collecting data that would document project outcomes. Nevertheless, one of the advantages of work in a rural community is the availability of anecdotal data, which will be briefly detailed in an effort to convey participants' perceptions of the value of the project.

The response of the families to the news of termination was universally one of profound disappointment. For months after being notified of the project's untimely ending, chance meetings between former participants and group leaders in the community would evoke expressions of regret from the families, as well as statements about how they were continuing to use their skills from the group in a variety of ways.

Although the group leaders had anticipated that families would increase their communication about sexual issues, they learned from families of other unanticipated outcomes. Two daughters who had been living apart from their mothers decided to return to their mothers' homes after both had participated in the project. Improved communication skills were cited as the reason for the daughters' readiness to reunite with their mothers, and the project experience was cited by all as instrumental in improving those skills. Parents of five teens who completed a volunteer training session and subsequently served as facilitators in the group commented on the self-confidence the experience had given these adolescents. Several parents who had been reported for child abuse told the group leader that they are now able to find nonviolent ways of expressing their emotions when family tensions rise. A number of parents told the group leaders that the project had sensitized them to the needs of their preteens in the area of sexual learning. Fathers, who comprised 30% of parent participants, indicated to group leaders that they are now much more comfortable speaking with their children about sexual issues.

In addition to anecdotal reports of changed behavior, several new social programs in the community could be attributed directly to the influence of the project. One adolescent, moved by discussion in an enrichment session on suicide, developed with six of her friends a peer counseling program in her school, with the enthusiastic support of the school administration. One group of families continued to meet informally for six months after the formal termination of the project, ultimately telling the group leader that they had successfully met their group's learning goals. One group leader was able to locate funding for work with community families, and 13 of her original 50 families became enthusiastic participants in the new project that stressed family communication skills. The second group leader found employment as a director of Christian education in a community church and proceeded to implement a program similar to the Family Life Demonstration Project. Both group leaders attributed their readiness to take programmatic initiative to the knowledge, skills, and administrative expertise they had gained in their year of experience with the project. As natural helpers in the community, they found new and creative ways of channeling their skills, thereby contributing to the community in an enduring way.

IMPLICATIONS FOR SOCIAL WORK PRACTICE

Programs stressing sexual learning have the potential to grow and flourish in rural communities, especially when natural helping networks are identified and involved from the initial stages. Although rural communities have a number of limitations that must be considered when developing new programs, these can be counterbalanced by utilizing the existing strengths: interest in social contacts, desire to make family life more satisfying, enthusiasm for skills that encourage self-sufficiency, and a commitment to improving life in the community as a whole. Social workers have always known the value of "starting where the client is." When it turns out that the client is an entire community, it is crucial to spend ample time learning about the unique attributes of that community and identifying natural helpers. As can be seen from the example of the Family Life Demonstration Project, rural families whose members feel involved and committed to a program need not allow the formal ending of that program to deter them from integrating new knowledge and skills into the more subtle helping relationships that are such a crucial part of the community's life.

REFERENCES

Andrews, D.D. & Linden, R.R. (1984). Preventing rural child abuse: Progress in spite of cutbacks. *Child Welfare*, *63*, 443-452.

Bedics, B.C. & Doelker, R. (1983). Mobilizing informal resources in rural communities. *Human Services in the Rural Environment*, *8*, 18-23.

Collins, A.H. & Pancoast, D.L. (1976). *Natural helping networks: A strategy for prevention*. New York: National Association of Social Workers.

D'Augelli, A.R. & Hart, M.M. (1987). Gay women, men, and families in rural settings: Toward the development of helping communities. *American Journal of Community Psychology*, *15*, 79-93.

Davenport, J. & Davenport, J. (1982). Utilizing the social network in rural communities. *Social Casework*, *63*, 106-113.

Dotson, D. (1979). Occupational health—organizing for the right to breathe. *Human Services in the Rural Environment*, *4*, 4-11.

Kirby, D., Alter, J. & Scales, P. (1979). *An Analysis of U.S. education programs and evaluation methods*. Bethesda, MD: Mathtech, Inc.

Mindick, B. (1986). *Social elements in family matters*. New York: Praeger.

Mindick, B. & Oskamp, S. (1982). Individual differences among adolescent contraceptors: Some implications for intervention. In I.R. Stuart and C.F. Wells (Eds.), *Pregnancy in Adolescence: Needs, problems, and management*. New York: Van Nostrand Reinhold.

Rose, S.D. (1973). *Treating children in groups*. London: Jossey-Bass Publishers.

Rounds, K.A. (1988). Responding to AIDS: Rural Community Strategies. *Social Casework*, *69*, 360-364.

Shapiro, C.H. (1981). Adolescent pregnancy prevention: School-community cooperation. Springfield, IL: Charles C Thomas, Publisher.

Shapiro, C.H. (1987). Comprehensive curriculum: Family life demonstration project. Ithaca, NY: unpublished.

Skaggs, K.G. (1971). Education for manpower: To serve the people better. In *National Growth: The rural component* (pp. 40-48). Washington, DC: Government Printing Office.

Yoder, D.R. (1980). Spouse assault: A community approach. *Human Services in the Rural Environment*, *5*, 25-28.

AIDS Education is Sex Education: Rural and Urban Challenges

Sylvia S. Hacker

SUMMARY. This article discusses the history of our restrictive attitudes toward sexuality, and suggests some requirements for moving beyond our outmoded norms. Such a process will enable professionals and other adults to handle the explicit educational approaches necessary for dealing with the connection between sexuality and AIDS.

INTRODUCTION

In studying the AIDS epidemic, epidemiologists see AIDS as occupying a social niche and then spreading to other niches (Wolcott, 1988). The first niche has been occupied by homosexual and bisexual men, with drug users providing the second niche. It is postulated that the third social niche is characterized by the young, sexually active adolescents who are experimenting with drugs. Despite the fact that studies show a decline in drug use by American youth, the *level* of use is still higher than in any other industrialized nation (Research News, 1987). Further cause for alarm is the evidence that sexually active adolescents tend to have multiple sex partners (Kegeles et al., 1988), and that the incidence of STDs has been rising unabated among young heterosexuals (Findlay, 1988).

That young people everywhere engage in high risk behaviors has been well documented (Becker & Joseph, 1988). This is not surprising since adolescence is characterized, not only by experimentation, but by a distinct sense of immortality. In the Kegeles (1988) study cited above, the sexually active adolescents, ages 14-19, demonstrated a high level of knowledge about the effectiveness of condoms in preventing STDs as well as a consensus that their use was of great value. Yet, despite the fact that the study was conducted in a large city, where media and school coverage of the AIDS epidemic was high, the use of condoms was very low. Two other recent surveys of young college students (constituting a population of older adolescents) revealed a high level of knowledge about AIDS and its modes of transmission. Again, among those indicating they were sexually active, in one study only 25% reported using safe sex methods, and about 30% did not know what safe sex methods were. In the second study, while there was an overall use of the condom of 33%, only 10% used it every time (Chervin, 1988; DiClemente, 1988). With such behavior among informed, urban young people, even more exposed than the high school population to AIDS information on campus, what should we expect from younger teenagers, or from those in rural areas where knowledge about AIDS and other STDs is much lower?

It seems clear that even if adolescents understand, in abstract terms, what behavior is necessary to protect them against STDs, and also feel that it is of value, they continue to feel personally invulnerable to contracting diseases from sex partners. It is therefore, necessary, and the focus of this paper, to address methods of reaching teens at a level that will be personally meaningful—that will talk more frankly than before about the actual behaviors in which they are engaging, i.e., multiple partners, specific sex practices, drug experimentation, bisexuality, etc.

Surgeon General, C. Everett Koop (Time, 1986) and all other experts in the area of sex education, recognizing that young people are going to be sexually active whether we like it or not, are saying that education is our only weapon right now for the primary prevention of the disease. The problem is that no one is really addressing the *kind* of education that is needed. It is simply not sufficient to merely deliver biological facts, or such preachments like "Just say no" to drugs and sex. The reason that sex education in the schools has not been effective is that 90% of the programs are still relentlessly teaching "plumbing," i.e., anatomy and physiology (Kirby, Alter & Scales, 1979). Because so much of the education is largely a matter of labeling the reproductive organs, it might humorously be referred to as an organ recital. Indeed such knowledge is important, but it should be properly labeled as anatomy and not sex education. Adolescents, even as young as Jr. High level, are asking, for example, "How much is normal?" (in regard to masturbation), "Is oral sex harmful?" "What do I do if he's pressuring me?" "At what age is it OK to have sex?" "What's an orgasm?" (often spelled, "organism"), "What do you do if you're horny?" and lately, more and more, "What's anal sex?" or "What are AIDS?" Since there are very few programs dealing with such explicit questions, there is a great deal of nebulous terminology that these teenagers pick up (no matter how protected they may be) and, without processing, it turns into myths and half-truths. As June Osborne, dean of the University of Michigan, School of Public Health, has stated (Wolcott, 1988)

> . . . to address those matters, we must use words that no one is supposed to use, and we must acknowledge that real life mores do not yield instantly to the admonition to just say "no." (p. 35)

We are living in a highly eroticized environment, bombarded constantly with sexual messages from TV, magazines and newspapers. Thus, it is inevitable that young people will absorb isolated pieces of information. However, without the opportunity to discuss or examine this information, there is confusion about what it all means, or how to behave. It is no wonder that we are in the midst of serious problems revolving around sexuality—a million teen pregnancies (about half of which are aborted), burgeoning levels of STDS, school dropouts, increasing child abuse and neglect by teen parents, etc. The New Right is blaming these problems on a breakdown in the family and in morality. Parents are blaming their young adolescents—"Why don't they listen to us? When I was a kid, I used to listen to my parents!" The young are blaming parents, and everyone is blaming teachers. Blame, however, is counterproductive. It keeps us from attacking the problems. The fact is that no one is really to blame. In order to understand the current problems, the failure to deal with them adequately, and the tendency to blame, it is helpful to examine all of this within an historical context.

OUR SEXUAL HISTORY

All societies develop norms for human behavior, and sexuality is one of those behaviors. The sexual norm under which our society operated prior to World War II was essentially:

SEX IS BAD, except in marriage, BUT PARENTHOOD IS GOOD.

Three basic premises incorporated under this norm were as follows:

1. Sex equals intercourse *only* (for purposes of procreation). The pleasuring aspects were totally ignored.
2. Children are asexual – they are innocent and know nothing until they reach puberty. Then the hormones begin to rage, and the family begins to push girls into early marriage, and boys into sports.
3. Sexual thoughts, emotions, and fantasies are equally as evil as sexual deeds. One was exhorted to think pure thoughts – to sublimate. Cold showers, reading intensively, sports, and needlework were considered good means of counteracting sexual urges.

This norm, which is essentially one of denial that we are sexual beings, worked for a long time, since all institutions and authorities (e.g., parents, churches, schools, and peers) reinforced it. After World War II, however, with rapid, unprecedented social change taking place, the power of these authorities began to wane. This phenomenon is not difficult to understand when one examines it according to Maslow's Hierarchy of Needs theory (1970). When a society is operating at the lowest levels of need, i.e., of survival and security (which is where ours was economically prior to World War II), the greatest effort is expended in simply making a living and keeping hearth and home together. At such times, group cooperation is high, and rules and regulations are strongly adhered to. When, however, those lower level needs are achieved, when food, clothing and shelter, and a sense of belongingness are present on a satisfactory level, attention can then be given to ego needs.

This country had unleashed an incredible technology in order to win the war, and applying it to peacetime endeavors launched us into an era of unparalleled prosperity. A large middle class was created which enjoyed a level of affluence never seen before. Affordable, comfortable housing and labor-saving devices contributed to more leisure time, and the post-war baby boom generation was provided, more adequately than any generation before, with their basic needs. Therefore, what emerged in the sixties was the "me" generation, the generation which declared, in the thrust to address ego needs, "I'm gonna do my own thing!" The ultimate goal, the top of Maslow's hierarchy of needs, is self-actualization, and an exciting era of adventure and individual growth was upon us.

In reaching for self-actualization, the quest to be everything one is capable of being, one had to explore new values and risk new adventures. Inevitably, old norms were rejected as being too limiting, too restrictive, and so the power of authority became eroded. Not unexpectedly, the old sexual norm was one of the first to be rejected since sex is a strong human drive that is difficult to control even under the strictest norms. Therefore, in a climate of "doing your own thing" it is not surprising that a rebellion would occur against restrictive sexual attitudes. The rejecters of the old norm, although well motivated, were at a disadvantage however. They had had no training in how to handle their sexuality, and no realization of the consequences of sexual exploration. As a result, the unwanted pregnancy and sexually-transmitted disease rates started to climb among youth until they reached their present epidemic level—distinctly now, a societal problem!

The new sense of freedom and exploration affected not only youth, but gave impetus to the women's movement and the civil rights movement. The development of the pill provided even greater energy to question old norms and to explore sexual options. However, having been reared under the old restrictive rules, the exploration was accompanied by little knowledge and by enormous guilt and shame. In addition, since old norms die hard, society has been very slow and reluctant to take action. What resulted, and what continues today, are two moralities side by side: the one which has encouraged more sexual freedom, and the other which is characterized by embarrassment and shame. As a result, teenagers are reluctant to anticipate upcoming intercourse because it is akin to "planning sin." However, unless such planning becomes acceptable, they will not take precautions against the well-documented health hazards associated with adolescent sexuality in this country. With the old norm still hanging heavily over our heads, professionals and parents, tending to shy away from embarrassing and difficult material, prefer to avoid the sexual issues.

The old norm of denial is clearly no longer working, but there is no new one to take its place. That is what is causing the confusion and the blaming. Many groups hold that we need to return to the old norm in order to solve the problems we now face. However, once freedoms are gained, they are not easily relinquished. Nor is it desirable to give up the positive aspects of the social changes such as greater women's rights or more freedom of choice in lifestyle and jobs. The challenge is to maintain the freedoms at the same time as we attack the problems, admittedly a very difficult task. However, if we can conceptualize what we should be working toward, we can begin to devise means of implementing it.

DEVELOPING A NEW NORM

At present, with the advent of AIDS, it is no longer acceptable to tolerate society's ambivalence about sexuality. The gravity of this health problem must, I believe, supersede certain community sensitivities. It is now a life and death issue which calls for a more concerted effort in attacking the problems. It seems imperative, therefore, to propose working toward a new sexual norm, no longer one of denial, but one of acknowledgement that we are indeed sexual beings. It means moving from a sex-negative attitude to a sex-positive one, which will be a struggle because the deeply ingrained messages that we carry around from the old norm will cause discomfort, embarrassment and even pain. This might be particularly true in the more rural areas of the country where the influences of the "big city" are slower to absorb. Yet, because of ever-increasing media exposure, and the growing phenomenon of metroplexes in which there is blurring of rural and urban boundaries, absorbing is ultimately inevitable. Thus, if we can accept the premise that knowledge is not harmful, wrestling with emerging value conflicts can be a challenge. The learning will be exciting, will open up new areas of knowledge, and will definitely not be boring!

The new norm being suggested may be conceptualized as follows: SEXUALITY IS GOOD BUT UNWANTED PARENTHOOD IS BAD. It will be noted that the word "sex" was replaced by the expanded word "sexuality." The old word, restricted to intercourse, is now enlarged to include *all* aspects of sexuality, and in saying that it is good, it is creating a climate of acknowledgement rather than denial. It entails the acceptance of three major principles:

1. We are sexual from birth—from the cradle to the grave. Our sexuality is an inextricable part of our identity. We, as human beings, are susceptible to all sorts of sexual stimuli and pleasure. Human beings around the world enjoy both solo and mutual masturbation, touching and exploring in pairs and in groups, oral and anal sex, loving with members of the same sex, and so on (Ford & Beach, 1980). Intercourse is merely a small part of the spectrum.
2. Children are sexual and have sexual feelings from birth. Recent evidence, in fact, indicates that the sexual response system is even apparent at 29 weeks gestation (Calderone, 1983). This knowledge has prompted me to enlarge the "cradle to grave" assertion to: "We are sexual from the womb to the tomb." In growing up, children are naturally curious and exploratory in regard to their sexuality, as they are about everything else.
3. All thoughts, feelings, and fantasies are normal. They are all possible, human, and therefore normal. It is not the thoughts or emotions, but the behaviors which need to be monitored. We may *think* and *feel* what we like but we may not *do* everything. Learning which behaviors are appropriate is the primary task of becoming an adult. That's what sex education should be about: learning how to live together respectfully with other human beings, and making informed choices about which behaviors are appropriate, and which are not. The principle around which this question should revolve is that of nonexploitation—what it means and how we must apply it in everyday living. This is the essence of morality!

SOME APPLICATIONS OF THE PRINCIPLES

The author has asked, in her address to young people, "Why do you have sex?" After much groaning and such stage whispers as "What a dumb question!" she will say, "Listen, I'm so old, I've forgotten—help me out." The answers from the boys include, "It feels good," "It's such fun," "Lots of pleasure," etc. The girls, of course, are declaring "For love!" They still don't feel free to admit they can enjoy it too. They have then been challenged with this question: "If it's for pleasure, how come almost no girl has an orgasm, and the boys have their biggest orgasm when they talk about the event in the locker room to their buddies?" This elicits gales of laughter because they know it's the truth. She will then continue, "If it's the pleasure you're after, intercourse is not what you want. AND, of the whole range of possible sexual activities, it's the biggest health hazard!" This frequently causes boos and hisses, and on one occasion, a Jr. High School girl retorted, with some angry impatience, "If you're so smart, what do you do if you get hot?" The young girl sitting next to her added, with a naughty gleam, "and juicy." This presents an opportunity to carefully and explicitly discuss the range of sexual activities, other than intercourse, from masturbation to homosexuality, backing it all up with research, anthropological and historical evidence, and all the knowledge to which we have a fundamental right but to which we have been denied access because of our puritanical heritage.

It is extremely important to emphasize here that *learning* about the range of sexual behaviors that human beings engage in does not mean having to *do* them. Education is not indoctrination. The idea is to admit that such activities exist and examine them for their appropriateness, their harmfulness, and their potential for exploitation. Only then can we make responsible decisions about whether we should or should not engage in them. This is particularly important for adolescents because they are at an age where, in struggling between childhood and adulthood, they need alternatives in order to make choices (Franzkowiak, 1988). For example, students ask many questions regarding the normalcy of masturbation. It should be made clear that masturbation is normal whether you do it or not. It does not constitute a recommendation, but the provision of knowledge that, if it is within one's value system, it is a healthy outlet. We may not lie, as we once did, about masturbation causing blindness, insanity or growth of hair on the palms. We must provide the facts and let young people know there is a choice. This is important when dealing with conservative families who worry about having more liberal values imposed upon their children in schools. We need to reassure them that in providing knowledge, we are not *im*posing values but rather *ex*posing the multiplicity of views and practices in our pluralistic society. The aim is to be able to have our own set of values, based on learning and reason, but to simultaneously respect another's point of view (Hacker, 1986).

With regard to the increasing number of questions from young people about anal sex, it is clear that they are hearing somewhere about this activity as an outcome of all the publicity about AIDS and homosexuality. Again, consistent with the premise that knowledge is not harmful but, in fact, leads to better decision making, they deserve an honest, informative answer. In a group of pre-teens the author met with recently, they were asked to write a question they had about sexuality before the discussion started. Upon collecting them and coming to the one on anal sex, a straightforward answer was called for to the effect that it was an approach to sexuality in which the erect penis is inserted into the rectum. One girl of 12 shrieked, "Oh, gross! Who would want to put anything into their butt?" This was, indeed, a challenge! The group was asked if any among them had younger brothers and sisters, and of course, a number of them did. They were then asked if any of these siblings ever put objects into their noses, ears or mouths. There ensued a lively discussion about choking on things, peas shoved up nostrils, pebbles in ears, etc. This was followed up by explaining that human beings, from early childhood, are very curious and exploratory creatures. They often poke into such body openings as ears and noses, and sometimes put things in just to see how it feels. When they get older and find other openings (generally covered by clothing), they may push objects into those, or have partners do so just for the pleasure of it. What we need to discuss and learn is what is OK to put in and what isn't. A description was given of the tissue lining the rectum and its delicate surface covered with blood vessels. If people are going to experiment sexually with anal intercourse (and it is done by straights, as well as gays), then they must be careful not to tear that delicate tissue. In regard to AIDS, the highest risk exists if there are two conditions present: a large dose of the virus, and a blood connection. If a male is a carrier of the virus, his semen will have a large amount of it, and if the rectal tissue gets torn and is bleeding, you have a blood connection. It, therefore, can be very risky to ejaculate into the rectum, and it is recommended that it be avoided.

This kind of discussion can then lead to the use of condoms for both vaginal and anal intercourse. It needs to be stressed that one doesn't have to have intercourse to enjoy sexuality, but if they're not going to listen to this message, they must learn the proper way to use a condom. Here, we must be explicit in our teaching because it is wrong to assume that young people know how. They need to know about leaving a 1/2" on the end (and sketches of an erect penis, with a condom on , are wonderfully helpful), and the importance of holding on to it when pulling out. When relevant, the author has suggested incorporating the condom into sex play. Young males she has talked to are very interested in having their partner put the condom on for them. Female teenagers who often say they aren't sure they want to "touch that thing," would benefit, along with the males, from having condoms passed around the room so they can touch and feel them. All this needs to be part of a course which also teaches about the naturalness and normality of body secretions and excretions. It is quite evident, from teens' reactions and responses, that they view the entire urinogenital system as dirty, smelly, and suspect in general.

Other components of frank discussions must include:

1. The hierarchy of risks in regard to AIDS. For example:

– although at present the highest incidence of AIDS is among gay men, it is not a homosexual disease, and it's not OK to be anti gay. The homophobia in our society stems from our puritanical heritage. There is a substantial body of anthropological and historical literature, as well as research studies to indicate that homosexuality and bisexuality are part of the normal range of sexual expression. Expanding on the Kinsey six-point scale (1953), the author has conceptualized a continuum wherein bisexuality is variegated and may make up as much as 80% of the general population. About half major in homosexuality and minor in heterosexuality to one degree or another and the other half major in heterosexuality and minor in homosexuality to different degrees. When, and to what extent individuals act on their potential depends on time in history, societal norms, personal circumstances, etc. (Hacker, 1984)

– the *very* high risk of IV drug use. One can emphasize the concept of the second and third niches referred to at the beginning of this paper.

– vaginal intercourse is considered a lower risk than anal. Although there is the possibility of tissue abrasion (which would produce a blood connection), it can be the result of insufficient lubrication or of forcible entry.

– oral sex, if it includes ejaculation into the mouth, also entails risk because of possible gum lesions.

2. The advantages of postponing intercourse and focusing, instead, on enhancing one's sensuality include:

– Eliminating the risk of pregnancy and STDs.

– The wonderful potential of becoming a great lover. This can be substantiated by the extensive work of sex therapists who successfully treat dysfunction by having clients concentrate on pleasuring and defocus from intercourse. Literature on spine-injured patients, and their ability to learn how to thoroughly enjoy sexuality without intercourse, offers further reinforcement.

3. Examination of the characteristics of our present-day culture in regard to peer pressure, living in the fast lane, etc. (Bateson, March 18, 1988)

Possible Reactions

It is not difficult to imagine the problems which can arise in considering the above suggestions. There will be resistance, particularly in the more geographically isolated areas of the country. After all, if we were to move to a norm of acknowledgement, we would have to accept all the pleasuring aspects of sexuality. Although, intellectually, we may be quite willing to grapple with such ideas, on a deep gut level there lingers the old suspicion that such sex play as masturbation, oral and anal sex, etc. is, somehow, dirty. Therefore, when the author has stated in her talks, and documented with research, that intercourse can be a health hazard, and has suggested that we consider alternative approaches in meeting our sexual needs, there is considerable discomfort. It is especially difficult to accept pleasuring when we think of teens engaging in those alternative (dirty) behaviors—they're still children! This reaction is understandable when we realize how deeply ingrained is our value that sex is legitimate only for procreation—all other exploration simply seems questionable in terms of morals.

SOME RECOMMENDATIONS

There is considerable evidence that parents have difficulty in talking to their teenagers about sexuality (N.Y. Times, 1986). This is understandable in light of their own socialization under the old sexual norm. It would therefore be extremely useful for social work practitioners, in dealing with parents, to exhort them to seriously consider the tradeoffs. Would it not be better to produce children who are training to be good lovers (with the potential bonus of learning something themselves) than to risk pregnancy and STDs, particularly the deadly AIDS! Adults are aware that teenagers are, and always have been, risk takers. That is how they make the transition into adulthood. Just saying "no" does not work. In fact, the more they hear "no" without reasonable explanation, the more it evokes a feeling of revenge. Teens need alternatives.

If parents and/or professionals have trouble entertaining the approach being suggested, at the very least let us entreat them to become, what Sol and Judith Gordon term "askable" (Gordon & Gordon 1983). This does not mean they have to be comfortable nor that they will have the answers, but it entails having two main characteristics:

1. the ability to discuss and defend their value system (based on a willingness to learn) in a respectful manner, and
2. the ability to recognize that other opinions exist and to really listen to another's point of view.

It is perfectly OK to go slowly, to take the time to entertain and process any new knowledge to which they expose themselves. In fact, going slowly is more consistent with rural inclinations. The idea is to try not to shun, too hastily, new ideas which may be different, but to discuss them with their teenagers, examine them carefully, and learn together. This is the essence of communication.

Evidence that such an approach works is in research which shows the following: teens, whose parents talk to them about sexuality throughout their development, tend to postpone first intercourse, and when they do become sexually active, they use birth control more than others (Allgeier, 1983). Here, parents are acknowledging the basic sexuality of their offspring and are unafraid to deal with it as they grow.

Further Evidence to Support the Concept of Acknowledgement

School-based clinics, which represent an acknowledgement by the community of teenage sexuality, appear to be having considerable success in various parts of the country. The first model clinic in St. Paul, Minnesota showed a 66% reduction in the student fertility rate as well as 35% decline in dropout rates (Family Education for Health, 1986). In Baltimore, Maryland, in an experimental sex education program which made birth control available next door to the school, it was found that girls participating refrained from sexual relations longer than those not engaged in the program (N.Y. Times, July, 1986). In Jackson, Mississippi, teen pregnancy dropped at least 50% in seven years since the opening of school-based clinics (Katz, 1986).

In other industrialized nations around the world, where there is higher acceptance of the sexuality of young people, the teenage pregnancy rate is half or less than ours. For example, the Netherlands, where birth control is available in the high schools and where sex education begins early, has the lowest teenage pregnancy rate in the world, along with a very low rape and child sexual abuse rate. And Sweden, which has had sex education in the schools since 1956, rivals the low pregnancy rate of the Netherlands. Furthermore, in neither country has there been any evidence of a breakdown in family values, nor a lack of career development (Wellbourne-Moglia & Edwards, 1986).

In the author's own extensive experience in speaking with teens and pre-teens there has been a growing awareness that a low level of embarrassment, use of humor (especially when there is discomfort), directness in dealing with their very frank questions, honesty in admitting when uncertain (or even uncomfortable) about some issues, and giving permission to look up information, will result in requests to spend more time with the speaker or counselor. There is a thirst for knowledge about sexuality, and a need to wrestle with the issues surrounding it. The most frequent evaluation received by the author by young audiences is, "she sure tells it like it is—get her back!"

CONCLUSION

Sexual learning is social learning from birth throughout life because sexuality is an inextricable part of our identity. Our task is to develop a sex-positive outlook because, if we can celebrate our sexuality, we will be positively disposed and motivated toward avoiding risks to so wonderful a possession. But to do this, we will have to take a deep breath, plunge in, and work together even if it means facing real life activities and using taboo vocabulary. AIDS is everyone's concern. It is transmitted primarily via drugs and sex. Drugs are easy to talk about but sex is not. Therefore, sex needs to be taken out of the dark closet and aired. From this will come a fresh perspective and the courage to make a crucial change toward expanding our narrow concept of sex into the broader concept of sexuality. In the words of Surgeon General C. Everett Koop (1986):

> Those of us who are parents, educators and community leaders, indeed all adults, cannot disregard the responsibility to educate our young. The need is critical and the price of neglect is high. The lives of our young people depend on our fulfilling our responsibility.

REFERENCES

Allgeier, A. (1983). Informational barriers to contraception. In D. Byrne & W. Fischer (Eds.), *Adolescents, sex & contraception*. Hillsdale, NJ: L. Erlbaum Assoc.

Bateson, C. (1988, March 18). Once again, the AIDS furor. *New York Times*, p. A35.

Becker, M., & Joseph, J. (1988, April). AIDS and behavioral change to reduce risk: A review. *American Journal of Public Health*, *78*, 394-410.

Calderone, M. (1983, May/July). Fetal erection and its message to us. *SIECUS Report*, XI (5/6), 9-10.

Chervin, D.D. (1988). The university and the prevention of sexually transmitted diseases. In *Transmitted diseases and society*. Palo Alto: Stanford University Press.

DiClemente, R.J. (1987, October). Drugs and AIDS: effect of disinhibition by alcohol and recreational drugs on college students' use of condoms. Paper presented at the meeting of the APHA, New Orleans, LA.

Family education for health. (1986, March). *Health Link*, *11*, 45-49.

Findlay, S. (1988, February 29). Has the threat been exaggerated? *U.S. News and World Report*, *104*, 58-59.

Ford, C., & F. Beach. (1980). *Patterns of sexual behavior*. New York: Harper & Row.

Franzkowiak, P. (1988). Life in the fast lane – Adolescent risk-taking as a major challenge to health formation. *New Universals*. Published proceedings of the Fourth International Symposium on Adolescent Health, Sydney, Australia.

Gordon, S., & J. Gordon. (1983). *Raising a child conservatively in a sexually permissive world*. NY: Simon & Schuster, Fireside Books.

Hacker, S. (1984, Spring/Summer). Morality and sexuality. [Letter to readers section.] *Journal of Sex Education & Therapy*, *10*, 7-8.

Hacker, S. (1986, Spring/Summer). Telling it like it is: A challenge to the field of sex education. *Journal of Sex Education & Therapy*, *12*, 13-17.

Katz, G. (1986, October). Birth control is in more schools. *USA Today*.

Kegeles, S., Adler, N., & C. Irwin Jr. (1988, April). Sexually active adolescents and condoms: Changes over one year in knowledge, attitudes and use. *AJPH*, *78*, 460-461.

Kinsey, A., Pomeroy, W., Martin, C., & P. Gebhart. (1953). *Sexual behavior in the human female*. Philadelphia: Saunders.

Kirby, D., Alter, J., & P. Scales. (1979). *An analysis of sex education programs, and evaluation methods*. Atlanta: Math Tech Inc.

Koop, C. E. (1986, October). *Surgeon general's report on acquired immune deficiency syndrome*. Washington, DC: U.S. Department of Health & Human Services.

Maslow, A. (1970). *Motivation and personality*. NY: Harper & Row.

Report hails sex education. (1986, July 9). *NY Times*.

Sex and schools. (1986, November 24). *Time*, *128*, 54-63.

The drug scene in America. (1987, March-April). *Research News, 38* (pp. 10-11). Ann Arbor, MI: University of Michigan.
Wellbourne-Moglia, A., & S. Edwards. (1986, November/December). Sex education must be stopped! *SIECUS Report*, XV (2), 1-3.
Wolcott, N.F. (1988, January/February). AIDS, the curse and courage. *Michigan Alumnus, 95*, 19-39.

Index

For Product Safety Concerns and Information please contact our EU representative GPSR@taylorandfrancis.com
Taylor & Francis Verlag GmbH, Kaufingerstraße 24, 80331 München, Germany

www.ingramcontent.com/pod-product-compliance
Ingram Content Group UK Ltd.
Pitfield, Milton Keynes, MK11 3LW, UK
UKHW022120190926
475702UK00013B/1546
9781138965973